Zionism
A Brief History

ר האט שוין פֿאַרגעסן,
ין גייט אין אַ ניים
לות!
עדיינק ייד, יעדער
לות פּירט צום
נמעגבאַנג.

Markus Wiener
Publishers

PRINCETON

שוין גענוג!
בוויל א היים!

Zionism
A Brief History

Michael Brenner
Translated by Shelley Frisch

Translation of the Yiddish text in the illustration
on the preceding two pages:

(New York)   (Palestine)
He has already forgotten   Enough already!
and goes to a new exile   I want to go home!
Remember, Jew,
each exile leads to destruction.

For information write to:
Markus Wiener Publishers
231 Nassau Street, Princeton, NJ 08542

Library of Congress Cataloging-in-Publication Data

Brenner, Michael.
  [Geschichte des Zionismus. English]
  Zionism: a brief history/Michael Brenner;
  translated from German by Shelley L. Frisch.
  Includes bibliographical references and index.
  ISBN 1-55876-300-7 (hardcover : alk. paper)
  ISBN 1-55876-301-5 (pbk. : alk. paper)
  1. Zionism—History. I. Title.
  DS149 .B84713 2003
  320.54'095694—dc21
  2002151806

Printed in the United States of America on acid-free paper.

Contents

Preface to the English Edition

The subtitle of this book is to be taken seriously: this is indeed a *brief* history of Zionism. There are numerous studies specializing in a variety of aspects of the Zionist movement and also a few detailed and lengthy historical accounts from the First Zionist Congress to the State of Israel. This book, however, is a comprehensive summary mainly intended as introductory reading about the topic. I hope it will spark interest in the further readings listed at the end of the book. Since this is not a book for specialists, footnotes are reduced to a minimum and sources provided only when quotations are used. Similarly, the bibliography contains only a selection of English-language literature, although there is of course a plethora of readings in Hebrew, German, and other languages.

When writing this book I discovered for myself what I always told my students: it is much more difficult to write a short paper than a long paper or, in this case, a short book than a long book. To restrict oneself to a limited number of pages means naturally to sort out the material with particular scrutiny and to leave out many things that are dear to one's own understanding and others that will be missed by the knowledgeable reader. The last section on the state of Israel is particularly affected by those restrictions. It is to be read as an epi-

logue, connecting some of the major issues of Israeli society to the history of pre-state Zionism, rather than as
a brief history of Israel.

It gives me special pleasure to thank those people
who made this volume possible. The students in my
classes on the history of Zionism and Israel at Indiana,
Brandeis, and Munich have often made me think
about topics that otherwise would have eluded me.
Michael Berkowitz, Michael A. Meyer, Derek Penslar,
Gideon Reuveni, and Bernard Wasserstein have read the
manuscript at various stages and commented exten-
sively. I have profited extremely from their suggestions.
Shelley Frisch was a first-rate translator and Markus
Wiener a most cooperative publisher. This book would
not have appeared in English without their initiative.

Munich, September 2002

CHAPTER ONE

The Early History of Political Zionism

Traditional Jews praying at the Western Wall in Jerusalem, 1873.

Few national movements have transformed the history of a people as radically as Zionism changed Jewish history over the past century. Initially it was dismissed or opposed by many Jews, and represented only one of several Jewish political movements. After the catastrophe of European Jewry, however, Zionism was regarded by almost all Jews as a symbol of hope for their continued existence. For some, the State of Israel, founded in 1948, became a new homeland; for others, it became an important point of orientation for their Jewish identity in the Diaspora. At the same time, rarely has a national movement had to fight as hard for its right to existence as Zionism, which was branded as a form of racism by the United Nations General Assembly in 1975. Although this same Assembly later repealed this resolution, the term Zionism is still greeted with hostility by some of its member nations. Israelis themselves have been debating for quite a while as to which ideological camp embodies "true" Zionism or whether Israeli society has reached a post-Zionist stage. Thus, even over half a century following the founding of a Jewish state, the term Zionism continues to be the subject of much discussion and political controversy.

Religious Origins

The origins of the idea of a Jewish return to the land that had been called Palestine since Roman times, but remained *Eretz Israel* (the land of Israel) in Jewish usage and was often identified with Mount Zion in Jerusalem, are as old as the Jewish Diaspora, for which the destructions of the two temples in Jerusalem in the years 586 B.C.E. and 70 C.E. were symbolic turning points. Mourning over Jerusalem and lamentations of exile have been captured most memorably in Psalm 137: "If I forget you, O Jerusalem, let my right hand wither. Let my tongue cleave to the roof of my mouth, if I do not remember you, if I do not set Jerusalem above my highest joy!" Over the course of centuries, Jews have prayed for a return to Zion. They have written poetry and actually made their way to the Holy Land. The Eighteen Benedictions, the core of the traditional Jewish prayer service, recited three times a day, envision a swift rebuilding of Jerusalem, as do the blessings at the table. The verses of the twelfth-century poet Yehudah Halevi, *Zion ha-lo tishali* . . . (O Zion! Will you not ask about the welfare of your captives . . .) are an extraordinarily moving document of medieval Jewish literature. The poet himself left Spain, the land of his birth, to go to Zion, and got at least as far as Egypt. It is probably just a legend that he died in Jerusalem, but it is certain that some members of the group of Jewish mystics from Eastern Europe that set out for Jerusalem in 1700 under the leadership of Rabbi Yehuda He-Chassid did make it to Jerusalem. Zionist historiography of the early twentieth century under the guidance of Ben-Zion Dinaburg (Dinur), who later became the Israeli Education Minister, regarded this first modern return movement as the beginning of modern Jewish history.

In his *Prehistory of Zionism*,[1] the Polish-Jewish historian Nathan M. Gelber meticulously researched these and other projects for a Jewish state that were proposed between 1695 and 1845. The proposals included extraordinary recommendations by Christians, such as one proposal by the Danish merchant Oliger Paulli in the early eighteenth century, who suggested that European Jews resettle in a Jewish empire to be established between the Black Sea and the Red Sea. All neighboring countries would serve as its fiefs. One century later, Napoleon entertained the idea of a project for a Jewish state, hoping that it would win over oriental Jews to his cause.

American Utopias

The most sensational proposition on the part of a Jew came from Mordecai Manuel Noah (1785–1851), a former consul of the American government for Tunis and high sheriff of New York. In 1825 ("in the fiftieth year of American Independence," as the end of his manifesto notes), he issued a proclamation to the Jews, which stated in part:

I have issued this my proclamation, announcing to the Jews throughout the world that an asylum is prepared and hereby offered to them, where they can enjoy the peace, comfort, and happiness which have been denied them, through the intolerance and misgovernment of former ages. An asylum in a free and powerful country, where ample protection is secured to their persons, their property, and religious rights; an asylum in a country, remarkable for its vast resources . . . "A land of milk and honey," where Israel may repose in peace, under his "vine and fig tree," and where our people may so familiarize themselves, with the science of government, and the lights of learning and civilation [sic], as may qualify them for that great and final restoration to their ancient heritage . . .[2]

This land is not situated where one might first expect it in light of the biblical allusions. Indeed, it lies far from any vines and fig trees, as we learn from Noah's subsequent description: "The desired spot in the state of New York to which I hereby invite my beloved people throughout the world, in common with those of every religious denomination, is called GRAND ISLAND, and on which I shall lay the foundation of a City of Refuge to be called ARARAT."[3] Grand Island, a stone's throw from Niagara Falls, is twelve miles long and three to seven miles wide. Noah proposed conducting "a census of the Jews throughout the world"[4] and levying an annual "capitation Tax" of three shekels of silver to finance the project for a Jewish state. He did not specify exactly who would be counted in this census; in his view the American Indians, for example, were one of the ten lost tribes. The Jewish state was slated to be proclaimed in a special ceremony on Grand Island on the first of Adar, 5586 (February 7, 1826). Noah was no idle observer of the event. He relocated to Buffalo, where he laid the symbolic cornerstone for his project on September 15, 1825 in St. Paul's Church, since there was no synagogue. The ceremonial entry into the church before the local dignitaries was accompanied by the Grand March from *Judas Maccabeus*, the opera by Jacques Halevy that had recently had its world premiere. The cornerstone with a Hebrew inscription was displayed on the communion table. Noah's action was followed by the international media and by Jews throughout the world, but was rejected from the start as an unrealistic venture. Anticipating the tenor of later disavowals of political Zionism by religious leaders, the chief rabbi of Paris explained that "only God knows the time of the return of the Israelites." Thus, Noah waited in vain and made his mark once again two decades later with a plan to return the Jews to Palestine.

Zionism and European Nationalism

Zionism could not take shape as a national movement until the era of European nationalism. The first modern concepts of a return movement to the Holy Land, which, it must be noted, still had strong religious

overtones, stemmed from regions that experienced national conflicts as early as the mid-nineteenth century,
namely the Balkans and the once Polish parts of Prussia.
In Semlin (Serbia), Yehuda Alkalai (1798–1878), a rabbi
born in Sarajevo, wrote a series of entreaties for the Jews
to return to Palestine. At the same time, in West Prussian Thorn, Rabbi Zvi Hirsch Kalischer (1795–1874) was
citing biblical and rabbinical texts in his *Drishat Zion*
(Seeking Zion, 1862) to demonstrate that the salvation
of the Jews would result from human efforts and would
not depend simply on divine providence in the Messianic Age. Kalischer contended that the colonization of
Palestine could begin at once. It is noteworthy that both
rabbis—one Sephardic (Alkalai was of Spanish-Portu-
guese descent) and the other Ashkenazi (Kalischer's origins were in Poznan)—who thought and argued so traditionally were profoundly affected by current political
developments. Alkalai regarded the traditional Jewish
idea of the first, temporary Messiah from the house of
Joseph not as an individual, but as a kind of Jewish
national collective. Kalischer recalled the European
events of mid-century when he counseled the Jews to
follow the examples of the Italians, Poles, and Hunga-
rians in their national struggles for freedom.

Alkalai and Kalischer stood not just at the center of
the conflicts between various nations, but at the very
crossroads of Jewish life between West and East. In
Central and Western Europe, a new definition of Jewish
existence on a purely religious basis had been develop-

Rabbi Yehuda Alkalai and his wife, around 1865

ing since the French Revolution and the beginnings of emancipation. Count Clermont-Tonnerre's pithy declaration before the French National Assembly of 1789, "The Jews must be granted everything as individuals— but nothing as a nation," captured the essence of the so-called emancipation contract of the Jews in all countries of Western and Central Europe. They were certainly entitled to become French citizens (and later German or Italian citizens), but would have to discard all national characteristics in the process and differentiate themselves from their fellow citizens only according to the religion that they practiced (or did not practice) on an individual basis.

Matters were altogether different in Eastern Europe, where the vast majority of the Jews lived. Here the state was only conditionally interested in the integration of the Jews as a religious minority, but the institutional prerequisites for a process of emancipation that were common in countries further to the West were lacking. Consequently, most Eastern European Jews retained collective traditions far beyond the religious domain into the twentieth century, notably a common language (Yiddish), education and culture, and often a style of dress that set them apart from others. They were concentrated in particular residential areas. Their explicit or implicit longing to return to the homeland of their forefathers also set them apart.

In Poland, Russia, Romania, or the Ukraine it would have been most unlikely for anyone to think of them as citizens of the Jewish faith. In these societies, in which social modernization progressed far more slowly than in Central or Western Europe, the Jewish community remained in some measure autonomous. Naturally it had also been strongly influenced by the intellectual, social, and political movements of its milieu at the end of the nineteenth century.

Poznan, West Prussia, and Serbia stood at the crossroads of these two Jewish worlds. The two most important Zionist writings in the decades preceding Herzl, however, would come from both sides of this crossroads. *Rome and Jerusalem* was the title of a short book by Moses Hess published in 1862. Two decades later, the Russian-Jewish doctor Leon Pinsker wrote a tract called *Auto-Emancipation* in direct response to the Russian pogroms. In 1896, when Theodor Herzl published *The Jewish State*, he had not read either of these books.

Moses Hess (1812–75) had already established a reputation in intellectual circles when he wrote *Rome and Jerusalem*. The inscription on his gravestone near Cologne was not far from the truth in calling him "the father of social democracy." A former comrade of Karl Marx, he first made a name for himself as a political writer. His anonymous work *Heilige Geschichte der Menschheit* (Sacred History of Mankind), which was published in 1837, is one of the early socialist writings in which both the Young Hegelian background of the author and the influence of the Saint-Simonists are evident.

Hess was one of many Zionists who pulled back from a universalist worldview to re-embrace particularism. He had to rediscover his Judaism, which he assumed he had long since shed. Herzl, Nordau, and Jabotinsky would later undergo the same process. The first letter of *Rome and Jerusalem*, which was written in epistolary format, opens as follows:

> After an estrangement of twenty years, I am back with my people. I have come to be one of them again, to participate in the celebration of the holy days, to share the memories and hopes of the nation, to take part in the spiritual and intellectual warfare going on within the House of Israel, on the one hand, and between our people and the surrounding civilized nations, on the other; for though the Jews have lived among the nations for almost two thousand years, they cannot, after all, become a mere part of the organic whole. A thought which I believed to be forever buried in my heart has been revived in me anew. It is the thought of my nationality, which is inseparably connected with my ancestral heritage . . .[5]

The essential elements that impelled the later founders of the Zionist movement are anticipated here: rediscovery of Judaism, redefinition of Judaism as a nationality and not as a religion, a long yet futile struggle for recognition and integration in the society around them, and emotional ties to the traditions and the homeland in the "ancestral heritage."

In addition, Hess's preoccupation with the "Jewish

question" is unquestionably related to the nationality conflicts of the mid-century. For *Rome and Jerusalem*, he chose the telling subtitle: "The Last Nationality Question," and wrote in the preface: "With the liberation of the Eternal City on the banks of the Tiber begins the liberation of the Eternal City on the slopes of Moriah; the renaissance of Italy heralds the rise of Judah. The orphaned children of Jerusalem will also participate in the great regeneration of nations, in their awakening from the lethargy of the Middle Ages, with its terrible nightmares."[6] For most readers, the title *Rome and Jerusalem* is likely to have suggested a religious work, possibly an analysis of the centers of Catholicism and Judaism. However, Hess was not referring to the Pope and the Jewish religion. He recognized earlier than most of his contemporaries that the so-called Jewish question was a problem not of religion, but of nation. His era was shaped not by conflicts between Christians and Jews, but between French and Germans, Jews and Germans, etc. Hess did not fail to note the racism that was making more and more headway: "The German hates the Jewish religion less than the race; he objects less to the Jews' peculiar beliefs than to their peculiar noses."[7]

The era was hardly amenable to the circulation of his book. Hess's former socialist associates dismissed his plan as the product of a perfidious dreamer. The majority of Jews who were intent on achieving integration and acculturation in the German states saw a distinctive ray of light at the end of the tunnel in the 1860s. After

the failed revolution of 1848 had at first destroyed their
short-lived legal equality, one state after another now
took up again the process of emancipation that had
been introduced half a century earlier. The orthodox
Jews, apart from exceptions such as Kalischer and Alkalai, still steadfastly refused to take upon themselves the
deeds reserved for the Messianic Age. Most Jews in
Eastern Europe were quite insulated at this point. It took
wave of pogroms in the 1880s to rouse them.

A New Beginning in Russia

The assassination of Tsar Alexander II in 1881 triggered a series of pogroms. The Jewish communities of
Tsarist Russia, already plagued by various forms of discrimination and a precarious economic situation, were
now subjected to physical violence as well. Leon Pinsker
(1821–91), a Jewish doctor from Odessa, the capital of
the Jewish enlightenment movement, reacted at once
with a theoretical tract. His pamphlet, called *Auto-
Emancipation* (1882), was written in German, which typ-
ified the Russian Jewish intelligentsia's quest for Enlightenment and his belief that the Jews' salvation
would come from the West. Pinsker's life resembled that
of many German Jews as early as the second half of the
nineteenth century, but in Russia it was atypical. The
fact that he had grown up speaking Russian (but knew
Hebrew as well), went on to study medicine in Moscow,

the capital city, and ultimately pursued the career he had envisioned as a respected doctor made him an exception among the Russian Jews. The shock of 1881 must have been that much more painful for Pinsker. As the title of his pamphlet indicates, he considered the path of emancipation ineffectual and called instead for the self-emancipation of the Jews as a nation in their home. In his view, this self-emancipation could occur only outside the boundaries of Europe. Pinsker did not initially specify where it would take place, and gave consideration to both Argentina and Palestine. The fact of the matter was that the overwhelming majority of the more than two million Russian Jews who left their homeland in the four decades following 1881 did not look to the Middle East, but rather to North America. However, at least a symbolic beginning to the modern Jewish settlement of Palestine had been set in motion, as we will see in chapter 3.

Politicizing Jewish Society in Western Europe

Settlement in Palestine was only one of numerous factors that highlighted the unparalleled transformation of Jewish society at the close of the century. At the beginning of the century, this populace had resided at the margins of society, generally in rural areas. In a very brief period of time, it underwent a transformation into

a middle-class urban group in Central and Western
Europe. Many became quite prominent in several areas
of economic and cultural life as well as in specific professional groups, notably doctors and lawyers. In
Eastern Europe, this process was artificially impeded by
government restrictions. However, it was universally accepted that the Jewish ghetto either had ceased to exist
or was in the process of dissolution, in terms of both
individual lifestyles and isolation from mainstream
society.

Zionism was one facet of a more general European
Jewish politicization at the close of the nineteenth century. Because of its long-term political success and the
catastrophe of European Jewry, people tend to forget
that at almost the very same time other specifically
Jewish political directions were evolving, such as the
socialist "Bund" ("Algemeyner yidisher Arbeter Bund in
Lite, Poyln un Rusland"), the Jewish autonomy movement, and new liberal organizations that focused on
integration as citizens of the Jewish faith.

This politicization of European Jewry began in 1860,
when the Alliance Israélite Universelle was founded to
support Jews in crisis throughout the world in reaction
to the so-called Damascus Affair of 1840 and the
Mortara incident of 1858. The Damascus Affair centered
on an accusation imported from Christian Europe into
the Muslim Orient, which contended that Jews in Damascus had killed a Christian child and used its blood
for ritual purposes. This medieval legend, long con-

signed to oblivion, now induced severe riots against Syrian Jews, and was initially taken at face value even by French diplomats. Respected British and French Jews, notably Sir Moses Montefiore and the later French Minister of Justice Adolphe Crémieux, hastened to point out the folly of accusations of this sort and provide help to Jews who were threatened. The Mortara incident involved the forced baptism of a Jewish boy in Italy; this baptism was subsequently approved by the Catholic Church. The boy was seized from his family by papal officers and raised as a Catholic, never to be returned to his parents. The Alliance, which was formed to provide assistance in similar cases and ultimately also served to raise the educational level of Middle Eastern and Northern African Jews by building up a network of French-speaking schools, provided the first modern international context for Jewish political activity.

The last decade of the nineteenth century ushered in a series of organizations dedicated first and foremost to the struggle against antisemitism. These organizations also explored the future outlook for Jews in a non-Jewish environment. The most notable example was the German Centralverein deutscher Staatsbürger jüdischen Glaubens (Central Organization of German Citizens of the Jewish Faith), which was founded in Berlin in 1893 and soon became the largest German-Jewish organization. The message was apparent from its name: the German Jews, who had acquired citizenship with equal rights when Germany was united in 1871, differed from their Christian fellow citizens only in the forms of their religious expression, which included visits to synagogues, cemetery statutes, religious instruction, and rabbinical training. But we might wonder why they would found their own association if these areas were already handled by the religious administration. The answer can be sought in a new type of political antisemitism that was flaring up in the early 1890s. The Centralverein was initially conceived as a defensive association against antisemitism, which experienced a hitherto unprecedented wave of popularity in 1893 when sixteen outspoken antisemitic delegates were elected into the Reichstag. Antisemitism had found its way into the 1892 platform of the German Conservative Party (the so-called Tivoli Program) and into newly-formed mass organizations, from the Bund deutscher Landwirte to the Alldeutscher Verband to the Deutschnationaler Handlungsgehilfenverband. It was therefore inevitable that a group that regarded itself as a religious community in response to how it was viewed by others would found an organization that was political. Over the course of the following decades, the Centralverein focused increasingly on questions of Jewish identity and put less emphasis on the defense against enemies from without. Regardless of whether they had intended this shift of focus, the German Jews at the beginning of the twentieth century thus had their own mass organization in the Centralverein, which represented them on a political level to the outside world.

Autonomists, Bundists, and Agudists in Eastern Europe

In Eastern Europe, secularization had resulted in the formation of a steadily growing intellectual class that was also seeking a new definition of its Jewish identity. This group was united by a common language and culture as well as by rejection from the surrounding society. The Jewish Enlightenment movement (*haskala*) revived the Hebrew language as a new medium for secular Jewish culture in Eastern Europe; its first forums were magazines, publishing houses, and intellectual circles.

In the course of politicizing Jewish life, the battle over language now took on a political dimension as well. The "Hebraists" were in accord with the assimilated Jews in at least one respect. Both condemned the "jargon," which is how they referred to the Yiddish language that was spoken by the Eastern European Jewish masses. They advocated the use of "pure" languages, as had Moses Mendelssohn at the beginning of the Jewish Enlightenment movement.

A counter-movement arose to promote the Yiddish language as the cultural language of the Jews. The representatives of this movement labelled the advocates of Hebrew elitists. Like the Hebraists, the "Yiddishists" held their own language conferences, which were also political events. The Hebraists were typically in the Zionist camp, while the Yiddishists generally opted for more autonomy within the countries in which they lived.

Along these lines, the historian Simon Dubnov founded an autonomy movement that advocated recognizing Jews as a national minority with commensurate legal protection. For the classic representatives of a national solution for minorities, such as the Austrian Social Democrats, the Jews were not a national minority because they lacked their own territory, but for Dubnov, this was all the stronger justification for a solution involving autonomy. The Jews, he argued, embodied a higher level of nationalism, since they, as the oldest nation in existence, had already transcended the early stage of territorial nationalism and preserved their nationality for centuries in the Diaspora. Dubnov's *folkspartey* was one of the smaller Jewish political groups, but its tenets enjoyed success after World War I in the newly-founded states of East Central Europe. A Jewish minority status was legally instituted in Poland and the Baltic states.

The Bundists, who considered socialism in combination with Yiddish culture the solution to the Jewish question, carried greater weight within the array of Jewish parties. The Bund was founded in 1897 in Riga, even before Russian social democracy. For the Bundists, the Yiddish language was initially just a vehicle to communicate socialist ideas. However, they soon called for the recognition of the Yiddish language and culture as the legitimate Jewish form of expression, in the same way that Poles spoke Polish and Ukrainians Ukrainian. Naturally this demand fell on deaf ears in most circles of the socialist movement, which held that only nations with their own territory ought to be granted a national minority status.

An additional political offshoot of early Zionism, which formed in the early twentieth century, was territorialism. This movement, led by Israel Zangwill, a writer who lived in England, called for a national home for the Jews. No location was specified for this home. Antisemitism and the threat that followed in its path made it necessary for the Jews to accept any territory they were offered, even in Australia or South America.

It must be added that in this climate of increasing politicization, even religious orthodoxy founded its own organization in 1912, the Agudat Israel. Like the Zionists and Bundists, it acted as an independent political party during the interwar years in Poland and sent its own delegates to the Sejm (Parliament). Agudat Israel was emphatically anti-Zionist, and its foundation should be interpreted in part as a reaction to the formation just a few years earlier of a small religiously oriented faction within the Zionist camp, the so-called Mizrahi.

Thus Zionism appeared on the political stage as one among several Jewish groups at the close of the nineteenth century. The fact that it would prevail within just a few decades as the only one of these parties could not have been predicted in 1900. The following two chapters will demonstrate that Zionism has to be understood within the wider frame of the national and colonial projects of the late nineteenth and twentieth centuries, but cannot simply be grouped with either of those projects. Of course there were echoes of the Greek, Italian, and Polish nationalism, but most Jews did not live in a clearly defined territory and did not regard themselves as part of a Jewish nation. Moreover, the purchase of land and its cultivation and settlement certainly paralleled colonial movements, but in the case of Zionism, one crucial element was lacking, namely a colonial power in the name and interest of which a foreign land would be exploited. Zionism cannot be understood as a modern political phenomenon apart from these unique circumstances.

CHAPTER TWO

An International Nationalism: The Topography of Early Zionism

Theodor Herzl looking down on the Rhine River from the balcony of Hotel "Three Kings" in Basel during the Zionist Congress, 1903.

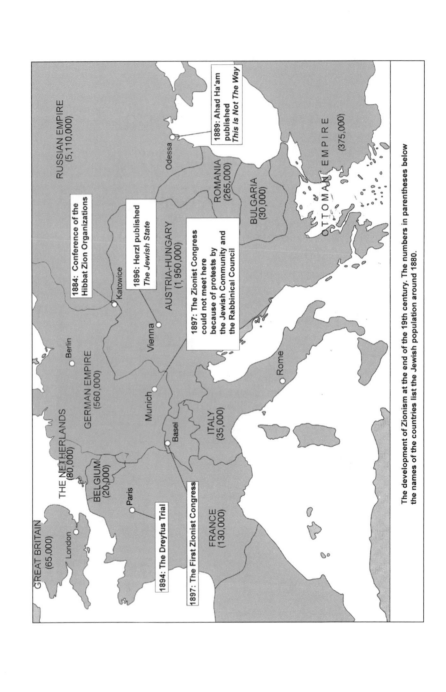

GREAT BRITAIN
(65,000)

London

THE NETHERLANDS
(80,000)

BELGIUM
(20,000)

Paris

FRANCE
(130,000)

GERMAN EMPIRE
(560,000)

Berlin

Munich

Basel

ITALY
(35,000)

Rome

RUSSIAN EMPIRE
(5,110,000)

Katowice

Vienna

AUSTRIA-HUNGARY
(1,950,000)

Odessa

ROMANIA
(265,000)

BULGARIA
(30,000)

OTTOMAN EMPIRE
(375,000)

1884: Conference of the
Hibbat Zion Organizations

1896: Herzl published
The Jewish State

1897: The Zionist Congress
could not meet here
because of protests by
the Jewish Community and
the Rabbinical Council

1889: Ahad Ha'am
published
This Is Not The Way

1894: The Dreyfus Trial

1897: The First Zionist Congress

The development of Zionism at the end of the 19th century. The numbers in parentheses below
the names of the countries list the Jewish population around 1880.

Regarding Zionism merely as an outgrowth of European nationalism would oversimplify the issue and ignore the international and cosmopolitan components of its genesis. The Jews did not merely lack a state and a territory in which the majority of them were concentrated. It was also a matter of controversy where the seat of the movement should be located, which language would be spoken at Zionist conferences, and where political allies could be found.

The map of early Zionism leads us through numerous cities of Europe. When people discuss the birthplace of Zionism, they usually refer to Basel. Theodor Herzl (1860–1904), the founder of political Zionism, wrote in his diary that he had founded the Jewish state in Basel. The first Zionist congresses took place in that city, and it was there that the Jewish movement gained international legitimacy. However, Basel was only the topographical termination point of a long series of places, each of which had a special role in the constitutive phase of Zionism. Vienna, for example, should certainly not be overlooked. Herzl was born in Budapest, but grew up in Vienna, and it was here that he established the first headquarters of the Zionist movement and published the first representative Zionist newspaper, *Die Welt*. Paris was an important city for Herzl because he covered the Dreyfus trial for the newspaper *Neue Freie Presse* in this city, and also because it was the adopted country of his right-hand man, the writer Max Nordau. Of the leading Zionists at the turn of the century,

Nordau was probably the best known. However, Paris also became a city of disillusionment for early Zionism. Theodor Herzl had placed high hopes for financing his project on Barons Hirsch and Rothschild, two philanthropists who lived in Paris. His overtures were summarily dismissed by both of them. Although they clearly recognized the threat to Eastern European Jews and supported their territorial and professional relocation to Argentina and Palestine, they wanted nothing to do with political plans that would lead to a Jewish state. Munich held a special place of honor in the long series of Herzl's political disappointments; in the summer of 1897, both the German Rabbinical Council and the executive board of the Jewish Community of Munich categorically rejected any plans to allow the first Zionist Congress to convene in the Bavarian capital.

This concentration on cities in Western and Central Europe has thus far disregarded the enormous significance of Eastern Europe for the formation of a mass movement. At the very least, we must include in our Zionist topography Odessa, which was the metropolis of an enlightened Eastern European Jewry and home of Leon Pinsker, of Herzl's adversary within the Zionist movement, Ahad Ha'am, and of the later founder of revisionist Zionism, Vladimir Jabotinsky. Our journey through Vienna, Paris, Munich, Basel, and Odessa ends in a place that existed only in the mind of Herzl. His utopian novel *Old New Land* (1902) was translated into Hebrew as *Tel Aviv* ("Hill of Spring"). This title became the name of the first Jewish city in Palestine. Of course Herzl would have to travel a long road in pursuit of that goal. We will now embark on a brief journey along that road.

Vienna

Let us begin our journey in 1878, when Theodor Herzl, who was then eighteen, left his birthplace of Budapest with his parents after the sudden death of his sister Pauline. For the Herzls, this move to Vienna meant crossing over from one half of the Habsburg dominions into the other. Austria and Hungary had been formally divided since 1867. The Herzls moved from Budapest, the capital of the Hungarian half, the culture of which had become increasingly Magyarized, to Vienna, the German-speaking capital. Theodor Herzl was a classic example of what we would now describe as an assimilated Jew. He grew up with no more than a rudimentary knowledge of the Jewish religion and culture. In sharp contrast to many of his Jewish contemporaries in Budapest, who identified with Magyarization, Herzl felt a close bond with German culture. His primary objective in Vienna, after initially following the wish of his parents and taking up the study of law, was to become a playwright at the Burgtheater. He had little to do with Jewish traditions. His parents had even refused to arrange a Bar Mitzvah ceremony in the synagogue when he turned thirteen, the religious age of adulthood, and later in life he did not have his son circumcised. His diary describes his original plans to solve the Jewish problem by means of a mass baptism of the younger generation of Viennese Jews. In December, 1895, he tried to win over the Viennese chief rabbi Moritz Güdemann to his basic Zionist tenets, but the latter recoiled even before entering Herzl's house when he caught sight of a Christmas tree there.

The move from Budapest to Vienna thrust Herzl into a new Jewish milieu, but his new home shared several features with the world he had left behind, for example the emancipation of the Jews in 1867. Both cities had rapidly growing Jewish communities: the Jewish population in Budapest increased from 45,000 in 1869 to 100,000 in 1890 and over 200,000 in 1920; in Vienna it grew from 40,000 to 120,000 to 175,000 in the same time frame. In both cases, these figures represented a significant percentage of the population (for the year 1890 in Budapest, roughly 20%; in Vienna, 8.7%). There was a high proportion of Jewish students in both cities around the turn of the century (in 1890, about 33% in Vienna and 50% in Budapest); the percentage of Jewish doctors and lawyers was even higher (over 50% in both Vienna and Budapest). Antisemitism was also inescapable in both cities.

Herzl's first encounter with antisemitism was as a seven-year-old in Budapest, as he later recalled. In Vienna, however, he would soon amass more extensive experiences. In order to compensate for the double stigma of his ancestry as a Hungarian and a Jew, he joined the pro-German fraternity Albia in Vienna. Herzl was one of the last three Jewish members accepted into the Albia; after 1881, no more Jews were admitted. Two years later, when Herzl was twenty-three, he left the fraternity after its blatant demonstration of antisemitism at a Wagner commemoration. The word antisemitic had been coined in the German empire shortly before, in 1879, and was popularized by the journalist Wilhelm Marr. In the so-called Berlin Antisemitism Debate of the same year, the court chaplain of Kaiser Wilhelm, Adolf Stoecker, and the historian Heinrich von Treitschke made this new term and all that it implied socially acceptable.

However, political antisemitism in the final decade of the nineteenth century was to enjoy its greatest popularity in Vienna rather than Berlin. Georg von Schönerer's German national antisemitism competed with the Christian Socialist antisemitism of Karl Lueger, and the latter emerged victorious. After achieving his first victory in the election of 1891, he captured an absolute majority of votes required by a complicated voting system in the May 1895 Viennese elections, and in 1897 he became mayor after Emperor Franz Joseph had refused to appoint him for two years.

Herzl's decision to become a Zionist was impelled by two distressing developments, namely his exclusion from several social circles and the intensifying climate of antisemitism in Vienna. A third factor was the growing distance with which he regarded the sophisticated Jewish bourgeoisie in Vienna. He wrote a series of shallow comedies to give literary expression to this feeling: *Muttersöhnchen* (Mama's Boy, 1885), *Wilddiebe* (Poachers, 1888), and *Was wird man sagen?* (What Will They Say?, 1889). After his resignation from the Albia and after Lueger's first electoral victories, Herzl began to add antisemitism to his literary themes. The crucial breakthrough in this process was *Das neue Ghetto* (The New Ghetto), a play he wrote in October 1894.

Das neue Ghetto was a critique of assimilation by an assimilated Jew. The Jewish bourgeoisie that Herzl portrayed featured social climbers and nouveaux riches, stockbrokers and speculators who lacked any sense of personal dignity and clung to the outer trappings of traditions that had long since eroded from within. They had forgone their Judaism without becoming Germans or Austrians. The play focused on Jewish internalization of antisemitic stereotypes and expressly criticized the process of emancipation and assimilation.

Herzl's characterization of assimilated Jews was quite typical for the Jewish intellectuals of his era. Herzl's longtime deputy at the head of the Zionist movement, Max Nordau, chose the same theme for his 1899 domestic tragedy *Doktor Kohn* (A Question of Honor). Herzl's and Nordau's critiques of bourgeois Jewish society were ultimately not so very different from what Theodor Lessing would later call *Der jüdische Selbsthass* (Jewish Self-Hatred, 1930). *Das neue Ghetto* must be understood

against the backdrop of a statement by Walther Rathenau from this same period (which Rathenau was later
loath to cite). Rathenau, who would eventually become
the German Foreign Minister, wrote in "Höre, Israel!"
(Hear, O Israel) in 1897: "Smack in the middle of German life is an isolated exotic race of men, shining and
strikingly dressed, hotblooded and constantly in motion. An Asiatic horde on the sands of Mark Branden-
burg . . . thus they live in a semi-voluntary, invisible
ghetto, not as a living limb of the nation, but as an alien
organism within its body." Rathenau, a German Jew,
asked "What needs to happen?" He suggested, as had
Herzl, "An event without historical precedent." However, his vision differed altogether from that of Herzl:
"Deliberate training of this race to achieve assimilation,
not in the Darwinian sense of 'mimicry,'. . . but by adap-
tation in the sense that both good and bad characteristics of the tribe be cast aside and replaced with others if
it is evident that they are inimical to their fellow countrymen."[8]

Walther Rathenau envisioned a patrician class of Jews
with the characteristics of Germans in the same year
that Herzl was dreaming of a Jewish state.

Although a text of this sort might appear to fall into
the classic genre "Jewish self-hatred," its author saw the
matter differently. He defended himself indignantly
against an allegation by his friend Alfred Kerr that he
was acting "inadvertently antisemitic." Rathenau's essay
was published—anonymously at first—in Maximilian

Harden's *Zukunft* (Future). Harden was born Felix Ernst Witkowski and serves as one of the six case studies of Jewish self-hatred in Theodor Lessing's book. Harden could get away with calling out to German Jews in his magazine: "What do you really want? You need to state clearly: whose business are you taking care of, the business of Germany or the business of Zion?"

Deep in his heart, Herzl kept hoping to belong to the dominant population, right up to the point of his Zionist awakening. His Zionist diary opens with a look back to 1893, when he sought to "solve the Jewish Question, at least in Austria, with the help of the Catholic Church."[9] In a ceremony he pictured down to every last detail, the younger generation of Viennese Jews would be led into St. Stephen's Cathedral and be baptized: "The conversion was to take place in broad daylight, Sundays at noon, in St. Stephen's Cathedral, with festive processions and amidst the pealing of bells. Not in shame, as individuals have converted up to now, but with proud gestures."[10] The important role he envisioned for himself and the love of detail that would characterize his later plans were already evident here: "As is my custom, I had thought out the entire plan down to all its minute details. I could see myself dealing with the Archbishop of Vienna; in imagination, I stood before the Pope—both of whom were very sorry that I wished to do no more than remain part of the last generation of Jews—and sent this slogan of the mingling of the races flying across the world."[11] He soon abandoned any plans to convert, realizing that a change of religion would do little to help since antisemitism was being defined racially. Jews might become Christians, but not Germans or Austrians. Even later, however, when he was already at work on his *Jewish State*, he aspired to belong to the upper crust of mainstream society. He noted in his diary on July 5, 1895: "By the way, if there is one thing I should like to be, it is a member of the old Prussian nobility."[12]

Let us imagine for a moment that Herzl had died one decade earlier and had tried to realize his plans for the mass baptism of the Viennese Jews shortly before his death. Possibly even Herzl would have gained admission to the inglorious gallery of Jewish self-haters that Theodor Lessing—who himself evolved from Jewish self-hatred to Zionism—compiled three decades later. In a letter to Harden, Herzl made it quite clear that he concurred with Rathenau's diagnosis, although he rejected the latter's remedy: "If he is advising the Jews to adopt a different bone structure, I will happily accompany him to this future of selective breeding. I am not poking fun at it, as any typical Jew would, but wish to concur with him. It is just that I think that the Jews will only be able to absorb the phosphorus for these new bones from a single source, namely from their own."[13]

Herzl diverged from Rathenau and Harden in the remedy rather than the diagnosis. In contrast to the aforementioned men, his dream of fleeing Judaism to join up with Christianity and consequently European society had been shattered by the time he wrote his drama *Das neue Ghetto*, which signalled his departure from the dream of assimilation. The final scene of the play makes a decisive about-face. Just like Max Nordau's *Doktor Kohn* a few years later, *Das neue Ghetto* ends with the death of the hero in a duel. In both texts, dueling is a symbolic act for the acceptance of Jews in a society that is less and less inclined to consider them equal partners. Jakob, the assimilated Jewish hero in Herzl's drama, is undone by the conventions of a society that refuses to accept him as one of their own. Before he dies, he expresses a sentiment that would now mark Herzl's own path. Clutching his mother's hand, he declares with his last ounce of strength: "O Jews, my brethren, they won't let you live again . . . Why do you hold me so tight? (*Mumbles.*) I want to get—out! (*Louder.*) Out—of—the—Ghetto!"[14]

Herzl had recognized in 1894 what many assimilated German Jews would finally be forced to acknowledge forty years later. The tragedy inherent in it was perhaps most poignantly expressed one generation later under altogether different circumstances by the painter Max Liebermann in a letter to the Hebrew national poet Chaim Nachman Bialik and the mayor of Tel Aviv, Meir Dizengoff, on June 6, 1933: "The revocation of equal rights is weighing heavily on all of us like a terrible nightmare, but especially on the Jews, who, like me, had cherished dreams of assimilation... As difficult as it was for me, I have awakened from the dream that I had dreamt my whole life."[15]

In order to assess Herzl's awakening from his dream of assimilation, we must first fathom his profound pain at the recognition of its futility: "Everywhere we have sincerely endeavored to merge with the national communities surrounding us and to preserve only the faith of our fathers. We are not permitted to do so. In vain are we loyal patriots, in some places even extravagantly so; in vain do we make the same sacrifices of life and property as our fellow citizens; in vain do we strive to enhance the fame of our native countries in the arts and sciences, or their wealth through trade and commerce. In our native lands where, after all, we too have lived for centuries, we are decried as aliens . . . If only we were left in peace. . . . But I think we shall not be left in peace."[16]

Paris

Although *Das neue Ghetto* is set in Vienna, Herzl had been living in Paris since October 1891 as a correspondent for the Viennese newspaper *Neue Freie Presse*. There has been considerable debate as to whether Herzl gathered the decisive experiences for his Zionist conversion in Vienna or in Paris, but one thing seems clear: the combination of Karl Lueger's triumph in the Viennese elections of 1895 and the conviction of the Jewish captain Alfred Dreyfus for high treason as well as the ensuing antisemitic street riots in Paris in December 1894 made it clear to Herzl which direction matters had to take.

The chronology of the events provides an interesting perspective. Herzl completed *Das neue Ghetto* on November 8, 1894. Edouard Drumont's antisemitic journal *Libre Parole* had already reported on Dreyfus's arrest on November 1, but the Dreyfus trial did not begin until December 19. Hence his later oft-repeated remark that the Dreyfus trial had made a Zionist out of him and that his play should be read in response to the trial should be taken with a grain of salt. However, it is incontestable that Herzl's four-year stay in Paris (until July 1895) really was a decisive point in his development as a Zionist.

France was the cradle not only of equality, liberty, and fraternity, but also of Jewish emancipation in Europe. The Jews in the German-speaking states were granted emancipation as a kind of reward for their successful assimilation to mainstream Christian society at the culmination of a process that had taken nearly a century to achieve (1867 in Austria, 1871 in Germany), but in France emancipation proceeded just the opposite way. As a consequence of the revolution, the Jews of France were first granted the same rights as their fellow Christians in 1790–91, and were then required to prove themselves worthy of it. Even after the German Jews had attained complete legal equality on paper, they were still far from it in reality. The Dreyfus scandal could not even have occurred in Berlin because non-baptized Jews were not allowed to become officers in the Prussian army until World War I.

This divergent development certainly did not mean that antisemitism was unknown in France, but it took a different form. In France, questioning the rights of the Jews also meant questioning the existing order. The fact that left-wing antisemitism blossomed in France during the first half of the nineteenth century may also be attributed to this disposition. Early socialists such as Charles Fourier, Alphonse Toussenel, and Pierre Joseph Proudhon identified the Jews with capital, as had Karl Marx in Germany in his early essay "On the Jewish Question." In the last quarter of the nineteenth century, of course, there was no lack of antisemitic slogans, defamatory writings, and political pamphlets in both countries. In France, Edouard Drumont's dreadful *La France juive* (Jewish France, 1886) achieved an enormous circulation. It was published in a popular edition in 1887 and in an illustrated version in 1892. Not even August Rohling's *Der Talmudjude* (The Talmud Jew, 1871) in the German-speaking countries could compete with it.

Theodor Herzl reported on French antisemitism for the *Neue Freie Presse* as early as 1892. He was certainly not naive enough to believe that no antisemitism existed in the cradle of emancipation. Nonetheless, the enormity of the events surrounding the Dreyfus Affair obviously astonished him. He was not the only observer in Paris to react this way. The French journalist Bernard

Lazare was, like Herzl, an assimilated Jew who had heaped criticism on his fellow believers, or, as we might say in his case, fellow non-believers. He initially sought to distinguish the German and Eastern European "Jews" from the French "Israelites." He wished to identify only with the latter, while distancing himself from the "Frankfurt money changers, Russian usurers, Polish bar-keepers and Galician pawnbrokers." In the prevailing climate of antisemitism he, too, changed his mind, and his sympathy for the plight of Jews grew. His 1894 study of antisemitism indicated that he too was moving toward a national Jewish solution. On November 17, 1894, just a few days after Theodor Herzl had complet-ed his *Neue Ghetto*, Lazare published an article called "Le nouveau Ghetto" in the left-wing Paris weekly *La Justice*. Although each undertook his writing project independ-ently of the other, they arrived at strikingly similar results. Lazare, in reaction to the arrest of Dreyfus, wrote: "The Jews are no longer confined to their own section of town . . . but they are imprisoned in a hostile atmosphere of suspicion, of latent hatred, of prejudice the more powerful for not being avowed, a ghetto far more terrible than that from which they could escape by exile or revolt. This hostility is generally concealed, but an intelligent Jew has no trouble perceiving it."[17]

Much of this covert hostility would become overt just a few weeks later. After the public degradation of Drey-fus, not only was the man who had been convicted—unjustly, as it later turned out—the target of the fury of the masses, but, as Herzl reported from Paris, the mobs on the street raucously shouted "mort aux juifs" ("death to the Jews"), which the assimilated Jewish editors of the *Neue Freie Presse* tried to render less inflammatory by rewording Herzl's text as "death to Judas." It was soon clear to both Herzl and Lazare that Dreyfus was serving as a Jewish scapegoat for the misdeeds of others. Even after Dreyfus was pardoned in 1899, intellectual circles continued to be split into Dreyfusards and anti-Dreyfusards. Many individuals, including many non-Jewish French people (notably Emile Zola), joined Lazare and Dreyfus' family by taking up the cause for justice.

In response to the Dreyfus trial, and probably to the first electoral victory of Lueger's Christian Socialists in the Viennese elections of April 2, 1895 as well, Herzl decided to stop observing the worsening situation of European Jews from afar. He was now determined to draw up a plan for action. In his quest for a financier for this plan, he turned to the well-known philanthropist Baron Maurice de Hirsch on May 20, 1895. This decision was carefully calculated. Hirsch, who was born in Munich and lived in Paris, had already proven his support of Jewish resettlement plans outside of Europe. His construction of a Trans-Balkan railroad network into Turkey was probably his most spectacular achievement. In order to bring the Jews out of Europe into safety and to transform them from merchants into farmers, he acquired land in Argentina and other countries in America for his Jewish Colonization Association. However, his grandiose plan to settle a total of 3 million Eastern European Jews in Argentina had attracted all of 3,000 people by the time of his death in 1896.

In a lengthy discussion with Hirsch, Herzl tried to convince him that the latter's own plans were doomed to failure, and that only the establishment of a Jewish state had any chance of succeeding. Hirsch would attract only beggars who lived off the generosity of the Baron, but Herzl would recast the Jews in a new mold along the lines of his sentiment in a posthumously published poem: "When will I know that my mission on earth has been a success? When poor Jewish youth become proud young Jews!" Many of the basic ideas he would soon be recording in his *Jewish State* are broached in his "Notes for a Meeting with Baron Hirsch," including his belief that it would not be necessary to relinquish Europe when emigrating to the Orient: "You are attached to your dreadful home? We will give it back to you in an embellished form. . . . We will build Paris, Rome, Florence, Genoa—whatever we want. Splendid cities that utilize all of the modern inventions. A state shielded from danger."[18]

As though he were rehearsing for a play, Herzl noted down precisely what he needed to convey. He recited and drilled his message, and presented it during his visit on June 2, 1895. This message concluded with an urgent appeal to the Baron: "This is how you can become the good Pharaoh, immortal in history, who has redeemed the people (who can no longer be burned)." All of his efforts came to naught. The conversation ended on a less than harmonious note, and the two never spoke again. The very next day, Herzl sent the Baron a long letter. This letter reveals the depths of his exasperation with Hirsch, whom he accused of "not even having had the patience" to hear out his ideas. By June 7, he considered this chapter of his endeavor over and done with: "Hirsch—a week ago he still was the cornerstone of my plans; today he has declined to a *quantité absolument négligeable* [completely negligible quantity], toward which I even feel magnanimous—in thoughts."[19]

There was only one more possible source Herzl could tap to finance his plans: the Rothschilds. This time he wanted to present a meticulously worded argument in writing from the outset. The notes he completed on June 17, 1895 became the first draft of his *Jewish State*, which appeared in print in 1896 and formed the basis of political Zionism. His remarks, entitled "To the Family Council," expanded into a grandiose concept, which he dared to compare to the exodus from Egypt. If Hirsch—or, later, Rothschild—played the good Pharaoh, it was clear who was assigned the role of Moses in this plan. This role was far more powerful than that of the biblical exodus: "The Exodus under Moses bears the same relation to this project as a Hans Sachs Shrovetide play does to a Wagner opera."[20] It was no coincidence that Herzl used the antisemite Wagner as a measure of grandiosity.

However, he awaited a meeting with the Rothschilds in vain. The chief rabbi of Vienna, Moritz Güdemann, whom he envisioned as the man who would establish contact with Albert Rothschild from the Viennese branch of the Rothschild family, was anything but enthusiastic, and he later rejected Herzl's Zionism in print. His friend Friedrich Schiff upset Herzl even more. When Herzl sought to test Schiff's reaction to his ideas, the latter interpreted them as a manifestation of a nervous breakdown, and felt that Herzl was in urgent need of convalescence. Herzl received similar negative responses from other people who were close to him. The single significant exception was Max Nordau, who, like Herzl, was born in Budapest and enjoyed great popularity as a writer in Paris.

After his return from Paris to Vienna in February 1896, Herzl published an expanded book version of his address to the Rothschilds, which he never had the opportunity to deliver in person. The book was entitled *The Jewish State: Attempt at a Modern Solution of the Jewish Question.* In contrast to his later utopian novel *Old New Land*, the Jewish State reads like a sober instruction manual for constructing a national homeland. After a brief analysis of the futility of all attempts at assimilation as well as the causes and effects of antisemitism, he began describing his plan, which would require the foundation of a "Society of Jews" and a "Jewish Company" to handle the financial arrangements. The question of the location of the Jewish state, perhaps in Palestine or Argentina, was left open: "The Society will take whatever it is given and whatever is favored by the public opinion of the Jewish people."[21] Most of the chapter headings attest to the pragmatic nature of the book: "Immovable Property Transactions," "Purchase of Land," "Workers' Dwellings," "Work Relief," "Guarantees of the Company," "Settlement of Skilled Laborers," and "Raising the Capital."

Herzl envisioned Palestine as a country almost without people for a people without a country. In contrast to Ahad Ha'am, he never really paid heed to the Arab residents of Palestine, and could not imagine that a later confrontation with them might present a major impediment to his endeavor. The claims of the indigenous population seemed insignificant to Herzl, who had grown up in the colonialist era. However, he did not have a chauvinist concept in mind, and most assuredly not a racist one, but rather a tolerant form of co-existence between Jews and Arabs. In *The Jewish State*, his logic ran as follows: "And should it happen that men of other creeds and other nationalities come to live among us, we shall accord them honorable protection and equality before the law. We have learned tolerance in Europe."[22]

Herzl's "Society" was not based on the model of the classic nation-state. It more closely resembled a voluntary amalgamation of interested parties. It is evident from his later writings that Arabs were also part of it, while some Jews—especially the ultraorthodox, whom he classified as fanatic—could live in Palestine without becoming members of the "Society."

He resolved the linguistic issues in a thoroughly European manner, following the Swiss model of "linguistic federalism."[23] He did not consider adopting Hebrew as the common language, because, as he remarked ironically, who could order a train ticket in Hebrew? All western languages would therefore be accepted in Palestine, but German would have a major significance and become the official language of the Zionist Congresses, in part because of its proximity to Yiddish, which was spoken by the Eastern European Jews. Herzl's Jewish state is a model of a progressive society and a social utopia.

The initial reactions to this little book, which had a print run of 3,000 copies, were anything but encouraging. After the book was given a lengthy review in the London *Jewish Chronicle*, letters began arriving from England that inquired whether the book's author was the well-known Viennese journalist. The secretary of the Viennese Jewish *Kultusgemeinde* (community) could not imagine that this book could have come from the very reasonable person he knew. Quite a bit of ridicule ensued back in Herzl's homeland. The critic Karl Kraus was bitterly sarcastic. In sharp polemics against Theodor Herzl and Zionism, he took up the allegation that the Jews were showing dual loyalty to a Jewish homeland and to their country of citizenship in Europe, and picked it apart with irony. Kraus accused the Zionists of responding to the antisemitic battle cry "Out with you, Jews!" with the reply: "Yes, out with us Jews!" According to Kraus, Herzl wanted to uproot the European Jews from their respective homelands. He made mincemeat of what he caricatured as Herzl's theory, namely "that the Jews were just staying on in Europe here and there to improve the tourist trade," and disputed Herzl's theory of a Jewish people: "After all, what common bond could unite the interests of the German, English, French, Slavic, and Turkish Jews into one political entity?"[24]

The two Jewish editors of Herzl's newspaper, the *Neue Freie Presse*, reacted to his publication with deathly silence. Not a word about this book or its author would appear in their newspaper. However, Herzl garnered support from a most unwelcome source. Many antisemites were tickled at the prospect that the Jews might now leave Europe of their own accord. This was the triumphant sentiment of Ivan von Simonyi, an antisemitic Hungarian member of parliament, who even made a point of paying Herzl a personal visit.

Munich

These were the very reactions that the circles of western assimilated Jews from Herzl's own milieu had been fearing. They protested that Herzl's book was providing ammunition for antisemitism. Herzl's analysis utterly contradicted the way they saw themselves. Judaism had been institutionalized in a manner that was analogous to mainstream Christian society. In order not to provide the opponents of emancipation with any weapons, these Jews defined themselves as a mere religious community.

Thus, the outcry was all the more enraged when Herzl wrote in *The Jewish State*: "We are a people, *one* people."[25] Quite possibly this sentence was the most provocative of his entire book, since it placed a century of emancipatory endeavors in question and cast Jewish self-definition in an antithetical new mold. Herzl contended that religion was no longer a bonding element, but a divisive one. As an assimilated Jew, he was himself the product of a rapidly progressing secularization. One generation Jews could be heard saying: "The fact that we go to the synagogue on the Sabbath and you go to church on Sunday is what divides us from you." Now, as some ironically remarked, it was more like: "The fact that we do *not* go to the synagogue on the Sabbath and you do *not* go to church on Sunday is what separates us."

However, Herzl knew that even those who did not set foot in a synagogue still remained Jews not only in the eyes of others, but also in their own self-image. Uniting all Jews, according to Herzl, was their common heritage, their history, and their marginalization by the society around them. He might never have become a Zionist if the Albia fraternity had continued to accept Jews, if there had been no Lueger in Vienna, and if no Dreyfus trial had taken place.

Herzl's plans were an outgrowth of nineteenth-century emancipation and assimilation. He accepted both processes and held out the hope that they would be carried through. In his view, emancipation had failed because the Jews retained individual rights, but no collective rights. The latter could be achieved only by the same means available to any other nation, namely within the context of their own state. In turn, he wanted to see the achievements of assimilation introduced in this state, which he envisioned as a Switzerland of the Orient. He had no desire to return to a pre-emancipatory era, but to extend emancipation outside of Europe while maintaining a European orientation. He was what was later often called a "post-assimilatory" Jew, so securely situated in the surrounding culture and society that he had no need to disguise his Judaism or to confine it to the religious framework of the synagogue.

When Herzl first brought these ideas to the public arena, he could still be dismissed as a literary journalist whose fantasies, just like those of Moses Hess and others before him, would never outlast the paper on which they were written. Herzl did not for a moment consider going down in history only as a theoretician of a new movement, but rather got straight to work making his plans a reality. Early in his diplomatic activities Herzl was received by the Grand Duke of Baden, who had little to offer beyond an exchange of pleasantries. To Herzl's disappointment, this visit did not open the door to the Grand Duke's nephew, the German Emperor, or

to the Russian Tsar, who was a cousin by marriage. A trip
to Istanbul did not result in a meeting with the Sultan,
as he had hoped, but Herzl was decorated with a Com-
mander's Cross of the Ottoman Medjidiye Order, which
he could claim as a mark of his success. With fevered
energy he set about organizing the first Zionist Congress. However, there would be no lack of hurdles on the
way to the Congress.

Vienna and Paris were the two most important stations on his path to Zionism. Munich was considered
synonymous with resistance from within the Jewish

Theodore Herzl and Max Nordau attacked by dogs barking, "I protest" and "Jews of yesterday" symbolizing the Jewish protest against the first Zionist Congress.

community. After giving initial consideration to holding the Congress in Zurich, he opted for the Bavarian capital because of the strong presence in Zurich of Russian secret police, who would instill fear in the Eastern European participants. In this matter Herzl was also clearly pragmatic. He was not seeking a venue that was significant in Jewish history or a large Jewish community, but rather an easily accessible locale. Munich failed to become the birthplace of political Zionism because of resistance of the local Jewish community and the German Rabbinical Council. This council, which comprised liberal as well as orthodox rabbis, whom Herzl derisively called the "protest rabbis," incorporated into its written resolution the two decisive arguments that could be heard time and again against Zionism. The resolution stated in part: "The aspirations of the so-called Zionists to establish a national Jewish state in Palestine contradict the messianic promises of Judaism as enunciated in the holy scripture and later religious canons."[26] Even today, for a large body of the ultra-orthodox, the founding of a Jewish state before the long-awaited Messianic Age and by secular Jews poses an irreconcilable conflict. It was the second point, however, that brought out the crux of their resistance: "Judaism obliges its adherents to serve the fatherland to which they belong with utmost devotion and to further its national interests with all their heart and strength."[27] The rabbis wanted to avert allegations of divided loyalty that were always being raised by the antisemites. It

was incumbent upon them to prove themselves loyal
German citizens of the Jewish faith.

Basel

When Herzl noted in his diary on February 14, 1896,
after the first 500 copies of his *Jewish State* were deliv-
ered: "My life may now take a new turn,"[28] he was
choosing an uncharacteristically cautious and modest
formulation. Within just a few months, Herzl became
known throughout the Jewish world as the undisputed
leader of secular Jewish nationalism. This recognition
ultimately stood him in good stead in running the Congress. He planned out and personally oversaw every
detail of this Congress. When Herzl had described the
planned mass baptism in the St. Stephen's Cathedral in
his early diary entries, he had imbued symbols with the
utmost consequence. The symbolic significance of the
event he was now launching in Basel was equally momentous. At the last minute, he altered the original conference site when it turned out to be a smoke-filled beer
hall, and rented the municipal casino instead. A digni-
fied setting was essential to prove to the world that
Zionism was a movement to be taken seriously. Just as
important was the appearance of the delegates, as is evident in the dress code Herzl prescribed: "One of my first
practical ideas, months ago, was that people should be
made to attend the opening session in tails and white

tie. This worked out splendidly. Formal dress makes most people stiff. This stiffness immediately gave rise to a sedate tone—one they might not have had in light-colored summer suits or travel clothes—and I did not fail to heighten this tone to the point of solemnity. Nordau had turned up on the first day in a frock coat and flatly refused to go home and change to a full-dress suit. I drew him aside and begged him to do it as a favor to me. I told him: today the praesidium of the Zionist Congress is nothing at all, we still have to establish everything. People should get used to seeing the Congress as a most exalted and solemn thing. He allowed himself to be persuaded, and in return I hugged him gratefully. A quarter of an hour later he returned in formal dress."[29]

Even though Herzl would never experience a resounding success in the theater, he did bring theater into politics with great aplomb. In contrast to his role in the Viennese Burgtheater, Herzl was the sole director in the Basel casino. He knew exactly how to captivate his audience. The more than 200 participants (including about 20 women) were not exactly the audience of his dreams: No one of note from the Paris, Vienna, Berlin, or London Jewish society attended, to say nothing of the Hirsches and Rothschilds. The only participant with a high degree of prominence was Max Nordau (1849–1923), one of the most widely read cultural critics of the time. His book *Die conventionellen Lügen der Kulturmenschheit* (Conventional Lies of Civilization, 1883) had been translated into fifteen languages, including Japanese and Chinese. Nordau's most influential literary product was *Entartung* (Degeneration, 1892), which not only created a term that would be frequently misused later, but also inspired an entire literature. At the Basel Congress it was, as Herzl noted, "my constant concern during those three days to make Nordau forget that he was playing second fiddle at the Congress, a role from which his self-esteem visibly suffered."[30] Nonetheless, he had no doubt whatever that only he himself could

Theodore Herzl addressing the Second Zionist Congress in Basel, 1898. Drawing by M. Okin.

lead the Congress: "Everything rested on my shoulders; and this is not just something I am telling myself, for it was proved when on the afternoon of the third day I left because of fatigue and turned the chairmanship over to Nordau. Then everything was helter-skelter, and I was told afterwards that it was pandemonium. Even before I took the Chair, things didn't click."[31]

Herzl was probably not wrong on this point. The indisputable high point of the Congress came when he took the stage. Arthur Schnitzler had admired Herzl's considerable oratorial skills and the aura he projected back when he was a student, when both of them were members of a Viennese academic library group called the Akademische Lesehalle. Pictures of the First Congress and eyewitness reports make it difficult to believe that Herzl was only 37 at the time. With his long black beard, he looked like one of those ancient Assyrian kings in old portraits, and his speeches reminded participants familiar with the Bible of prophetic passages. Attendees reported that Herzl was feted like a king, and he himself used the language of prophecy in his diary: "Were I to sum up the Basel Congress in a word—which I shall guard against pronouncing publicly—it would be this: At Basel I founded the Jewish State. If I said this out loud today I would be answered by universal laughter. Perhaps in five years, and certainly in fifty, everyone will know it."[32] He noted down these words on September 3, 1897. A little over fifty years later, the State of Israel was founded.

Odessa

The absence of the Western European Jewish upper class from the upcoming Congress was eating away at Herzl when he noted in his diary on August 23, 1897: "Fact is—which I conceal from everyone—that I have only an army of *schnorrers* [beggars]. I am in command only of boys, beggars, and prigs."[33] Those gathered in Basel were not really beggars, but respected doctors, lawyers, journalists, writers, and eleven rabbis from twenty countries from Algeria to the United States. Sixty-three delegates came from Russia alone, and parts of the western delegations also consisted of Russian Jews studying and working in other countries. It became amply clear that the true emphasis of the new movement lay not in the west, but east of Vienna. Until World War I, the group of men who headed the Zionist Organization, notably Herzl, Nordau, David Wolffsohn, and Otto Warburg, continually moved between Vienna, Paris, Cologne, and Berlin. However, the heart of the movement was in Odessa, Warsaw, Pinsk, and Minsk. After the Congress Herzl no longer thought of them as an army of beggars, but declared full of admiration: "I had to remember how people had often objected in those early years: 'You will only win over the Russian Jews for this cause.' If they were to say this to me today, I would reply: 'That is enough!'"

Odessa was certainly not the most important community in Eastern Europe, nor was it one of the oldest.

However, in the nineteenth century it became the most influential center of *haskala*, the Jewish Enlightenment in Eastern Europe. The influence of western culture was in stronger evidence here than in many other cities of Tsarist Russia. In the year of the First Zionist Congress, 140,000 Jews lived in Odessa and constituted more than one-third of the local population. After Warsaw, Odessa was the second-largest Jewish community in Tsarist Russia. A combination of a firm grasp of traditions, the urban nature of the community, an economic upswing due to industrialization, and relatively modern educational systems prepared the basis for the genesis of a new intellectual Jewish class that was influenced by Russian culture and sought new ways of expressing its Jewish identity. The pogroms of 1871, 1881, and especially 1905, when over 300 Jews lost their lives, impelled the cultivated Jewish class to seek new paths for the future.

This was the ideal breeding ground for the genesis of a Zionist movement, the core of which formed in Odessa when Theodor Herzl was still trying to gain acceptance by the dueling fraternities. Moses Leib Lilienblum (1843–1910) called for the restoration of Israel in the land of his forefathers and paved the way for reviving the Hebrew language. Chaim Nachman Bialik, N. H. Rawnicki, and other prominent authors who wrote in Hebrew would later make their homes in Odessa. In the 1890s, important Hebrew periodicals were published here that had no equal elsewhere. Here it was that Leon

Pinsker proclaimed the "auto-emancipation" of the Jews in reaction to the 1881 pogroms. Pinsker was also significally involved in the attempt to unite the loose groups of those interested in emigrating to Palestine (the Hovevei Zion circle) into a political movement. As a successful doctor, modern enlightener, and political visionary, Pinsker certainly enjoyed great respect. However, he lacked the charisma necessary for mobilizing a political mass movement.

In the intellectual circles in Odessa there was only one commanding presence who could hold a candle to Theodor Herzl. That was Asher Ginzberg (1856–1927), the Hebrew writer better known by his nom de plume Ahad Ha'am ("one of the people"). He had been a Zionist long before Herzl discovered Zion. His own claims to leadership as well as his fundamental differences of opinion with Herzl about the essence of Zionism made it impossible for him to defer to Herzl, who was regarded as an "upstart" in matters of Zionism. He therefore traveled to Basel as an observer rather than a delegate. After his return, he described his position there as follows: "Even in Basel . . . I sat alone among my brothers, a mourner at the wedding banquet." His skepticism regarding Herzl's attempts to achieve the goals of Zionism by means of diplomacy and not by "false hope and imminent redemption" added fuel to the fire during the Congress. During the years to come, this difference of opinion ripened into an open conflict between the two leading representatives of the new movement.[34]

The contrasts between Herzl and Ahad Ha'am can be summarized as follows: Although both Herzl and Ahad Ha'am concurred that the Jewish state ought not to be a religious state, Ahad Ha'am focused on a revival of Hebrew culture as the center of the new Jewish society. By contrast, Herzl envisioned "Not a Hebrew state—a Jewish state where it is no disgrace to be a Jew."[35] Herzl was determined to save the Jews from physical harm: "Our movement is born of affliction, the affliction of Jews throughout the world."[36] Herzl sought to save the Jews, Ahad Ha'am to save Judaism. For the latter, Herzl's plan was nothing but assimilation on a collective basis. He continually posed the question: What is Jewish about Herzl's Jewish state? Rejecting Herzl's attempt at an immediate political solution, he insisted on a necessary preliminary stage of establishing a cultural center in Palestine from which the revival of Jewish culture in the Diaspora could proceed. In contrast to Herzl, Ahad Ha'am considered it practically feasible for only a small percentage of the Jewish people to settle in Palestine. Everyone else would receive new inspiration from this place. For Herzl, the failure of assimilation was the greatest disappointment, but for Ahad Ha'am the crucial danger lay in the potential success of assimilation and the disintegration of Judaism that would ensue.

The early years of these two great men of early Zionism could not have been more different. Herzl joined a German fraternity; Ahad Ha'am founded the secret order B'nai Moshe, which sought to achieve its major

goals in the land of Israel. Herzl wrote light comedies for
the Viennese stage while Ahad Ha'am was contributing
critical essays to a newly-created Hebrew press. When
Herzl went to Paris, Ahad Ha'am traveled through
Palestine.

Herzl was a pragmatist whose diplomatic efforts distinguished his type of Zionism as political Zionism,
whereas Ahad Ha'am, who was at pains to achieve an
intellectual center, was identified with the concept of
cultural Zionism. First and foremost, of course, Ahad
Ha'am was a critic who kept a close eye on the development of Zionism. In addition to his criticism of Herzl,
he devoted his energies to an examination of the earliest Zionist endeavors. Ahad Ha'am's first venture as an
author was an incisive analysis of the failings of the Hibbat Zion ("Lovers of Zion") movement; he called this
essay "This Is Not the Way" (1889). He insisted that the
foundation be laid first so that the country could be
built up, otherwise any efforts would be for naught.
Following his first trip to Palestine in 1891, he published an essay called "The Truth from Palestine," which
roundly criticized the conditions in the settlements that
had already been founded. Ahad Ha'am was also one of
the first Zionists to warn of tensions with the Arab population.

Tel Aviv

The contrasts between Ahad Ha'am and Herzl emerged again and again, but did not come to a head until after the publication of Herzl's *Old New Land* in 1902. Nahum Sokolow, one of the leading Russian Zionists, translated the novel into Hebrew. In this novel, Herzl envisioned an idealized society in which Jews and Arabs live together in peace and harmony. This society draws on the best the European countries had to offer: English boarding schools, French opera houses, and of course Austrian coffee and pastries. Perhaps most symbolic of any of Herzl's remarks was his proposal to design the state flag with seven stars as a symbol of the seven hours of the working day. In *Old New Land*, women enjoy complete equality, including the active and passive right to vote, which was unknown in Europe at the time. Electric street lamps hang from the palms "like big glass fruits," a revolutionary innovation at the turn of the century. Herzl felt no need to point out that the native Arab population would not offer any opposition to this politically and socially perfect system.

European culture, social achievements, co-existence with the Arab population . . . we may wonder where the Jewish religion fits into this scheme. In *Old New Land*, Herzl provides the answer: it is banished onto the Temple Mount. The astonished reader learns of Herzl's vision of a rebuilt temple: "Once more it had been erected with great quadrangular blocks of stone hewn from nearby quarries and hardened by the action of the atmosphere. Once more the pillars of bronze stood before the Holy Place of Israel. . . . In the forecourt was a mighty bronze altar, with an enormous basin called the brazen sea as in the olden days, when Solomon was king in Israel."[37] Exactly what this altar was intended to signify was unclear, since *Old New Land* never mentions animal sacrifice. All in all, Herzl's idea of the temple more closely resembles a Viennese synagogue than it does Mount Moriah, on which, according to Jewish tradition, Solomon's temple stood. The women pray in the gallery and the temple seats are sold according to the view they offer. On Friday evening, the "Lecha Dodi" is chanted to the accompaniment of a lute rather than an organ. Herzl filled his temple, as he had so much else, with his favorite symbols. From St. Stephen's in Vienna to the temple in Jerusalem, there is a long but straight road that a critic rooted in traditional Judaism could register only with shock and ridicule. "On what site was the Beth Hamikdash [the temple] really built?" Ahad Ha'am asked in amazement, because the Dome of the Rock towers above the Temple Mount even in Herzl's vision: "Ought we to believe that the 'old gray Samuel' . . . would have permitted construction at some other place? In *Old New Land* nothing can surprise you. Everything is one big marvel. . . . There is only mechanical mimicry, lacking any sense of national initiative."[38]

It is a subject of heated discussion today which vision, Herzl's or Ahad Ha'am's, more closely approximates the reality of the State of Israel. Generally Ahad Ha'am is regarded as the more liberal and realistic of the two. His sober assessment of Arab reactions and opportunities for immigration and particularly his more reserved and muted personality are always contrasted with Herzl's grandiose plans featuring a fantastic array of detail as well as his naive hope that the indigenous population would welcome the immigrants. It is clearly significant that the western Jew Herzl is identified with western imperialism and colonialism, while the eastern Jew Ahad Ha'am is perceived as part of a populace threatened by pogroms in Eastern Europe.

This contrast surely contains the proverbial grain of truth, but probably not much more than that. Herzl's *Old New Land* reminds the reader not only of the fantasy literature of a Jules Verne and the utopian visions of an Edward Bellamy, but also of cosmopolitan ideas that were all the rage at the turn of the century among many writers, and to a lesser degree among politicians. The Hungarian Jew Herzl, who felt just as much at home in Austria as in France, probably had no choice but to develop a cosmopolitan national concept in *Old New Land* that differed fundamentally from other nationalisms. This concept may have put off Ahad Ha'am, but for leading early Zionists it was representative. The early Zionists kept moving from one European country to another, speaking and writing in several languages, and gathering their inspiration for a future Jewish society from a highly diverse set of European models, as many of their life stories serve to illustrate.

The second man behind Herzl, who tellingly changed his name from "Südfeld" (southern field) to "Nordau" (northern meadow), came from Budapest, lived in Paris, and wrote books in German. He felt at home in many European societies, as did the leading spokesmen for Eastern European Zionism, Chaim Weizmann (1874–1952), Nahum Sokolow (1861–1937), and Leo Motzkin (1867–1933). Weizmann, who had studied in Germany and Switzerland, settled in England, where he made important discoveries as a chemist for his adopted homeland. Sokolow, who was born in Poland, spoke and wrote fluent Yiddish, Hebrew, Polish, English, German, and French. He was the editor of the Zionist journal *Die Welt* in Cologne, then moved to Berlin and eventually settled in England. Motzkin, who came from the Ukraine, studied in Berlin, headed the Zionist office in Copenhagen during the First World War, and was active in the Jewish delegations at the Paris Peace Conference after the war.

Paradoxically, the founder of the nationalist wing of the Zionist movement, Vladimir Jabotinsky (1880–1940), had the most cosmopolitan background. After growing up in Odessa's international atmosphere, he studied law in Bern and Rome and after a brief return to Odessa became the editor of several Zionist publications in Istanbul. During World War I, he organized the Jewish Legion in England. He translated Edgar Allan Poe and Dante into Hebrew, as well as poetry collections from French, Italian, and English. The theater in Odessa performed two of his Russian dramas. Later he translated the Hebrew poetry of Chaim Nachman Bialik into Russian.

Early Zionism was thus a national movement with a cosmopolitan background. The biographies of its leading figures and the constant shift of its centers from Vienna, Cologne, and Berlin to Copenhagen and eventually London are just as representative of it as Herzl's utopian novel *Old New Land*.

CHAPTER THREE

From Vision to Reality: Jewish Emigration to Palestine

This poster, printed in Prague in 1930, depicts the new ideal of a Zionist pioneer defending Jewish settlement with a sickle in one hand and a rifle in the other. The caption calls for "defense–security–construction" and quotes Nehemiah 4:17: "With one of his hands wrought in the work and with the other hand held a weapon."

Although Herzl may have founded the Jewish state in Basel, he certainly did not invent Zionism. There were already nineteen Jewish settlements in Palestine when he convened the Congress. In his immediate neighborhood, Vienna, the term "Zionism" had first appeared in print in 1892 in the writings of Nathan Birnbaum (1855–1920), who had established a journal called *Selbstwehr* (Self-Defense) in 1885. A full three years before he began publication of this journal, Birnbaum had gained prominence with Kadimah, the first national Jewish student organization. Also in Vienna, the journalist Peretz Smolenskin was the editor of the prominent Hebrew journal *Hashahar*. However, both Birnbaum and Smolenskin had roots in Eastern Europe. Smolenskin was from Odessa, and Birnbaum's journal had been inspired by Leon Pinsker's appeal for "auto-emancipation." As was the case in other Jewish national organizations, Kadimah's primary contingent was Eastern European students.

The "Old Yishuv"

The mass exodus of Jews from Tsarist Russia following the murder of Tsar Alexander II in 1881 resulted in a transposition of the numerical center of Jewish life from one continent to another within less than half a century. Of course the great majority of the emigrants journeyed not to the Middle East by way of the Mediter-

ranean, but to America by way of the Atlantic. A stream
of about two and a half million Eastern European Jews
gave the United States the largest Jewish community
after World War I. By contrast, the number of Jews who
left Eastern Europe to go to Palestine during the same
years, roughly 70,000, was more like a thin trickle.
Additionally, many of them left their new home once
again after finding that they could not deal with the
adverse living conditions, the trying economic situation, and the unfamiliar climate, which caused health
problems. America, the *goldene medine* (Yiddish for "gol-
den land"), offered alluring opportunities for a new
beginning. This country had been shaped by immigrants. Moving to Palestine meant sacrificing individual
economic and upward social mobility for the idea of a
new type of collective. Although the numbers of immigrants to Palestine stood well behind those who came
to America, the ensuing transformation of the Jewish
world was ultimately of even greater significance.

Immigration brought about a conspicuous change
in the character of the Jewish population in Palestine.
Over the past few centuries, a small Jewish group, later
known as the Old Yishuv, had been living in Palestine;
it was concentrated in the four holy cities of Jerusalem,
Hebron, Tiberias, and Safed. This group essentially lived
on *halukka* ("distribution"), money that had been collected for it in the Jewish Diaspora. Since living conditions in Palestine were far from comfortable, but settlement in the Holy Land was considered a religious com-

mandment, contributing *halukka* for one's brothers and sisters in Eretz Israel was regarded as a duty.

The wave of immigrants that began to arrive in the final decades of the 19th century, however, decried the system of *halukka*, calling it propagation of an unproductive lifestyle. They insisted on normalizing Jewish life, especially by transforming a merchant society to a society of farmers and returning from the city to the "soil." Idealized social notions of this sort were widespread in Eastern as well as Western Europe and were not limited to the Zionists. The first phase of agricultural settlements in Palestine began in 1870 with the foundation of the agricultural school Mikve Israel southwest of Jaffa. Additional settlements would soon follow, financially underwritten by initiatives on the part of the Rothschilds and Baron Maurice de Hirsch. They were administered in Paris by such institutions as the Alliance Israélite Universelle and the Jewish Colonization Association. These groups were developing similar plans in North and South America, and wanted nothing to do with Herzl's political plans for a Jewish state.

Thus, for the history of Zionism, a new chapter in the settlement of the land really began with the "New Yishuv," the emigration initiated by the members of the Hibbat Zion in Eastern Europe. The immigration movement between 1881 and 1904 (particularly 1882–84 and 1890–91) known as the "First Aliyah" (which literally means ascent) was widely regarded as a failure, while the true foundations of the Jewish society of Palestine were laid in the context of the Second Aliyah (1905–1914), the ideology of which was mainly Socialist-Zionist.

As is often the case with historical simplifications, further distinctions are warranted here. The Old Yishuv, which comprised about 25,000 people in 1870, was in large part not very old at all, but consisted of many Jews who had immigrated as recently as the mid-nineteenth century from Europe as well as from Yemen and other parts of the Arab world. The immigrants of the First Aliyah after 1881 had no background in agriculture and were still heavily dependent on support from the Diaspora, as had been the case for the Old Yishuv. However, the majority of the 40,000 immigrants of the much-vaunted Second Aliyah left the country again by the end of World War I.

In the early 19th century, only 10,000 Jews lived in Palestine, the total population of which stood between 150,000 and 300,000, according to various estimates. The largest Jewish community numbered 4,000, in Safed in the north of the country, where it also constituted a majority of the local population. In the course of the century, Jerusalem became the center of Jewish immigration. In 1880, before the First Aliyah began, the approximately 17,000 Jews made up the majority of the population in Jerusalem for the first time in centuries. In 1840, they had numbered about 5,000. Smaller communities had formed in Haifa and Jaffa as well. Most of these immigrants had resettled in the Holy Land for reasons of tradition and religion. Their goals had little in common with those later advocated by the Zionists. Statistics compiled in 1877 revealed that about one-third of the Jewish population of Jerusalem consisted of rabbis, teachers, and other community officials, and an additional fifth depended on charity. Eretz Israel may have always seemed like a cohesive country in the minds of the Jews, but under Ottoman rule it did not make up a political unity. Judea, the coastal strip from Jaffa southward, and the northern Negev belonged to the Sanjak of Jerusalem. Samaria constituted the Sanjak of Nablus, and Galilee the Sanjak of Acre. Until 1894, all of them were part of the province of Beirut. In that year, Jerusalem was separated from Beirut and granted a semi-autonomous status. The land east of the Jordan belonged to the province of Damascus.

The Two Immigration Waves Preceding World War I

1881 was a crucial year for the continued development of Palestine. Anti-Jewish pogroms threatened the existence of the largest Jewish community of that time and required an immediate and radical solution. Emigration societies were founded in many communities.

A foundation myth about the modern Jewish settlement of Palestine sprang up around an emigration group in the Ukrainian city of Kharkov, consisting pri-

marily of university students who called themselves
Bilu, derived from the Hebrew initial letters of a verse in
Isaiah (2:5): *Bet Yaakov lechu ve nelcha* ("O house of
Jacob, come ye, and let us go"). Initially these *Biluim*
had high hopes, and even pictured bringing 3,000 of
their followers to Palestine within half a year. Several
hundred sympathizers did in fact join up with them,
but they were unsuccessful in obtaining financial back-
ing from the Jewish establishment. Finally, in early
1882, sixteen of them set out for Istanbul devoid of any
financial resources, appropriate equipment, and, most
important of all, any idea of what would await them at
the end of their journey. Thirteen young men and one
woman began the next lap of their journey across the
Mediterranean on June 30, 1882, and after a brief stop
in Cyprus disembarked in Jaffa. An additional forty to
fifty Biluim followed them, but the extremely rugged
conditions of farming, illness, and infighting about the
correct way to build up the land meant that by 1884,
two-thirds of them had left Palestine.

Discussions of Russian immigration since the 1880s
often overlook the fact that a further decisive influx
came from neighboring Romania. Here the legal status
of the Jews was especially precarious, since according to
Romanian law, it was not possible to be both a Jew and
a Romanian citizen. Thus, the fourth-largest Jewish
community in Europe at that time, with a quarter of a
million people, lived as stateless people in their homeland. Romania's anti-Jewish policy did not improve

even after the intense diplomatic pressure exerted by the western powers during the 1878 Berlin Congress, which included a set of conditions laid down in print. On the contrary, when complete sovereignty was recognized, discrimination against the Jews reached a new height. The Romanian Jews' hope of putting international guarantees into practice had been dashed in the process. The result was a mass migration, which brought every fifth Romanian Jew to the United States between 1881 and 1910. As was the case in Tsarist Russia, a small percentage of the emigrants left Romania for Palestine. Romanian Jews founded Samarin, one of the first agricultural settlements (later called Zikhron Ya'akov), some 15 miles south of Haifa.

The Hibbat Zion movement, which originated in Eastern Europe, had not succeeded in developing an effective organization. Although more than 130 Hibbat Zion organizations were formed in Tsarist Russia between 1882 and 1890, and in 1884 they even convened an international conference in Prussian Kattowitz (Katowice), where they would not be observed by the Russian secret police, they did not manage to agree on a practical organizational structure. Equally fruitless were their attempts at a systematic construction of the new society in Palestine. During the period of the First Aliyah, twice as many Jewish agricultural colonies were established by Baron Hirsch's Jewish Colonization Association in Argentina as by the Zionists in Palestine. Moreover, these colonies were still usually employing Arab

manual laborers. Like the Old Yishuv, the First Aliyah
relied heavily on the financial and administrative support of institutions such as the Alliance Israélite Universelle and the Jewish Colonization Association. Thus,
the First Aliyah represented a wave of emigration that
was less effective in creating an organizational or political foundation for future settlement in Palestine than
in marking a symbolic beginning in the creation of agricultural cooperatives, the use of the Hebrew language,
and particularly the forging of a new self-definition as
part of a national emergence.

A second decisive period for emigration to Palestine
began in 1904–5. With the death of Theodor Herzl in
1904 and the choice of his successor David Wolffsohn as
the head of the Zionist movement, political Zionism
was evolving into practical Zionism. Herzl felt that Jewish mass settlement would only make sense after a successful diplomatic mission, but the practical Zionists
attempted to jump the gun by rapid settlement and
land purchases. A turning point that may have proven
still more significant was the failed Russian revolution
of 1905, which revealed to many Jewish socialists the
futility of struggling in Russia and fueled their enthusiasm to create a classless society in a land of their own.

Between 1904 and 1914, about 850,000 Jews emigrated from Eastern Europe to North America. During the
same period, the Jewish population of Palestine increased from 50,000 to just 80,000. Despite this rather
modest immigration, the course was set in the decade

preceding World War I in terms of both leadership and ideology for the future development of the Jewish population of Palestine. The future leadership of the Zionist workers' movement, which dominated Jewish political life in Palestine in the 1920s and 30s and thereafter provided the political elite of the young state of Israel, immigrated for the most part in the years before the First World War and had a similar social background. This was true of both the later prime ministers David Ben-Gurion (1886–1973) and Levi Eshkol (1895–1969) and the later presidents Yitzhak Ben-Zvi (1884–1963) and Zalman Shazar (1889–1974), and for numerous other members of the socialist establishment such as Berl Katznelson (1877–1944) and Yitzhak Tabenkin (1887–1971). Most were born in the 1880s, typically in relatively small cities of the Ukraine or White Russia, distinguished themselves by their cultural commitment as journalists, historians, or writers, and initially worked as agricultural workers after their immigration to Palestine. Although they were products of the socialist traditions in Russia and subscribed to socialist Zionism, they developed an understanding of democracy that tolerated other approaches and advocated an open party system.

This group regarded itself as an elite not only within the society of Palestine, but also within the Second Aliyah itself. David Ben-Gurion may have been exaggerating when he stated that only ten percent of the men and women of the Second Aliyah had remained in Palestine. However, it does appear correct that a major-

ity did leave the land to move on to America or to return to Europe. The reasons for this are apparent. The
immigrants' travel accounts and diaries bore witness
to the extraordinarily difficult living conditions facing a
population group accustomed to European standards.

An exception to the Russian Jewish domination of
Zionist activities in Palestine was the Prussian-born
Arthur Ruppin, who traveled to Jaffa in 1907 as head of
the Palestine Office of the World Zionist Organization.
During the following three decades, he had a decisive
role in building the Jewish society of Palestine. His
memoirs are testimony to the conditions he encountered. When Ruppin contracted typhus and required a
stay in a Jerusalem hospital, he pronounced this hospital "the parody of a medical institution, lacking running
water, a sufficient stock of linen and utensils, and
trained nurses."[39] The hospital received a few thousand
francs from the Rothschild family each year, which
enabled it to stay open in the summer "as long as possible, usually for three to four months. Then it was closed
again."[40] Thoroughfares were virtually non-existent,
with the exception of the railroad lines from Jaffa to
Jerusalem and Haifa to Tzemah. The roads were in abo-
minable condition; a car trip from Jaffa to Haifa took a
day and a half. In the only hotel along the way, fleas
and bedbugs awaited hapless travelers.

Ruppin certainly did not emigrate out of desperation.
As a young law clerk, who had just completed a doctorate in economics and had won the prestigious Heckel

Prize in Germany, he had a promising career ahead of him before deciding to leave. His diary described his resettlement in the following way: "It is quite clear to me that this emigration will decide my whole future. Either I shall find a suitable field of work in Palestine, and then my life's task will be the creation of an autonomous Jewish community there, or I shall become convinced that this idea is impracticable and live out my life as a lawyer in Berlin or its vicinity, perhaps occupied with biological research on the side, which would not be an unpleasant life, but in the last analysis an unsuccessful one for me."[41]

Ruppin was not a Zionist ideologue, but a pragmatist. Under his leadership in the years before and after the First World War, an infrastructure was established that would set the course for the country until the transformations set in motion by the primarily middle-class Third Aliyah from the Poland of the interwar period. Institutions such as the Palestine Commission, the Anglo-Palestine Bank, the Palestine Land Development Company, and in particular the Jewish National Fund (JNF) had one major goal: to purchase as much of the land of Palestine as possible for the Jewish population.

New Ways of Life: Agricultural Labor and the Hebrew Language

In the years preceding the First World War, two crucial foundations were laid for the future of Jewish society in Palestine: on a rural level, the kibbutz as a collective way of life, and on an urban level, the first large-scale Jewish city, Tel Aviv, founded in 1909. The first collective settlement of *kibbutz* (literally "gathering"), then called *kvutza*, was established in 1910 in Degania. Here, at the edge of the Sea of Galilee, ten men and two women transformed their economic ideal of a collective community into reality. Kibbutz members took charge of their own affairs autonomously, without any outside supervision or administration. The first kibbutzim were conceived as small units of 20 to 50 members who wished to break away from traditional bourgeois ways of life. At issue were not only rejection of private property, capitalist means of earning a living, and urban lifestyle, but also the structures of the nuclear family. Ought children to live with their parents or in a collective children's house in the kibbutz? Could women participate in the same agricultural duties as men, and were they entitled to equal rights in the administration? Did the kibbutz need to be self-sufficient and provide for all basic needs? These were some of the questions that both defined and split the kibbutz movement in its early years. Since a consensus could not always be reached, several courses began to develop in the kibbutzim, which grew in popularity particularly after World War I. In the 1930s, the largest of them, such as Yagur and Givat Brenner, had swelled to several hundred members, and in 1941, the benchmark of 1,000 was exceeded for the first time. The by then more than 25,000 members of the kibbutzim made up approximately five percent of the total Jewish population of Palestine.

The ideals of work and ties to the soil were central to the ideology of the Second Aliyah. These ideals were memorably formulated by Aaron David Gordon (1856–1922), who had come to Palestine in 1905 and worked on the land. He was sharply critical of the common practice of employing Arab workers on the agricultural colonies, and felt that this practice would only perpetuate the Diaspora way of life in the new homeland. The necessary regeneration of the Jews could come about only through the work of their own hands: "Work is the strength of the nation—with the strength of his labor the worker shall produce what the nation as a whole needs, what in reality is needed for the creation of its life and for the spirit of its life. . . . A people that was completely divorced from nature, that during 2000 years was imprisoned within walls, that became inured to all forms of life except to a life of labor, cannot become once again a living, natural, working people without bending all its will-power toward that end. We lack the fundamental element; we lack labor, but labor by which a people becomes rooted in its soil and in its culture."[42]

The ideal of reviving the Hebrew language was similarly vital to this generation of immigrants. Hebrew had never been forgotten, since it was the language of prayer, but it had not been employed in everyday use for many centuries. The reconstruction of Hebrew was achieved primarily by the Russian Zionist Eliezer Ben-Yehuda (1858–1922), who produced a new Hebrew dictionary. His insistence on speaking Hebrew had unintentionally ironic touches in its early stages. When he ordered his family to speak only Hebrew after immigrating to Palestine in the late 19th century, his young son fell altogether silent until he was five years old. A few years later, he snubbed his father when the latter handed him a copy of his own Hebrew translation of *The Count of Monte Christo* with the cutting rejoinder: "Thank you, Papa, I have already read it in French." Since Eliezer Ben-Yehuda did not have the most important basic terms of the modern language at his disposal in the late 19th century, the Hebrew spoken in his home was woefully inadequate. If, for example, he asked his wife, who understood very little Hebrew anyway, for a cup of coffee, his own vocabulary lacked the words for cup, saucer, spoon, and pour. His son Itamar Ben-Avi later recalled Ben-Yehuda gesticulating while saying: "Take that and do that and bring me that and I'll drink."[43]

Speaking Hebrew appeared to remain nothing but a utopian vision for Western European Zionists. Theodor Herzl never mastered the language, and the most popu-

lar German Zionist, Martin Buber, would not speak Hebrew even when appearing before the Hebrew cultural
convention in 1909. By contrast, Jewish writers of Eastern Europe, like Micha Yosef Berdichevsky (1865–1921),
Saul Tchernichovsky (1875–1943), and Yosef Chaim
Brenner (1881–1921), wrote in the Hebrew language,
and called for a transvaluation of all Jewish values that
sounded downright Nietzschean. They wished to create
a new Jewish outlook that had nothing to do with the
Jewry in exile of past centuries. Brenner, A. D. Gordon,
Shmuel Yosef Agnon (1884–1970) (who later spent over
a decade in Germany), and other prominent writers in
Hebrew had come to Palestine from Eastern Europe during the Second Aliyah. The swift Hebraization of the
Jewish population of Palestine was more cause for cele-
bration for an idealist like A. D. Gordon than the "conquest of labor," which was proceeding more slowly. Gordon's 1913 letter to Yosef Chaim Brenner summed up
the situation as follows: "You need only go back 30
years and look at the evolution of the Hebrew language
in Eretz Israel since then to be amazed at this mighty
phenomenon. Hebrew schools in the full sense of the
word, a real Hebrew high school . . . , many Hebrew-
speaking families, everyday Hebrew on the streets, in
stores, and so forth, Hebrew meetings, lectures, theater
performances, learning colloquial speech by listening to
others use it as an everyday occurrence, an almost universal understanding of the language—in short, a Jew
who speaks none of the languages spoken here other

than Hebrew can satisfy his linguistic needs using
Hebrew with little or no difficulty. Who would have
thought so thirty years ago? Who in all honesty would
have dared to dream of such a thing?"[44]

The plan to make Hebrew an official language in the
modern educational institutions did arouse some controversy. After the first academic institutions had been
established in Palestine—a teachers' training college
founded in 1904 in Jerusalem, the first Hebrew-speaking
Jewish high school in Jaffa one year later, and Bezalel,
an art academy in Jerusalem—an intense debate on language erupted in 1912, when the Hilfsverein der deut-
schen Juden founded a technical college in Haifa on the
condition that instruction would be in German. When
the teachers at this and other Hilfsverein schools protested its linguistic policy, a separate Hebrew-speaking
school system was created; by the beginning of World
War I, it numbered over 3,000 pupils.

Even after Hebrew had become established as the official language of the Jewish population in Palestine,
Yiddish, Ladino, Russian, and other languages were still
heard on the streets. Arthur Ruppin confessed a full 30
years after his immigration how sketchy his command
of Hebrew was; it would remain so even though he took
private lessons from the future Nobel Prize winner S. Y.
Agnon. When he visited agricultural settlements at the
beginning of his time in office, he spoke in German.
Even when he later lectured in Hebrew, his background
was hard to miss. When a Prussian chief administrator

who understood no Hebrew attended one of these lectures, Ruppin reported: "But when I began to speak Hebrew, he was unsettled and astounded. Finally he could no longer refrain from turning to his neighbor, Dr. Hantke, and declaring: 'Hey, what is that? I almost understand that! That man must be from Magdeburg!' He had picked up the Magdeburg dialect in my Hebrew."[45]

When the eminent Zionist Martin Buber announced that his lecture on the occasion of a visit to the recently founded Hebrew University in May 1927 would be held in German, there was a storm of protests by professors and students. Buber did not change his mind, claiming that his Hebrew was simply too halting for a public lecture. A few years later, the protests became more militant, and enjoyed greater success in rallying against the planned establishment of a chair in Yiddish Language at the Hebrew University. A professorship in this subject in Jerusalem was inconceivable until long after the founding of the State of Israel. Even then, Yiddish was generally regarded in Israel as the embodiment of the ghetto and exile, more as "jargon" than language, but because Eastern European Jewry had been largely destroyed, Yiddish no longer posed a real threat to the Hebrew language.

The Path to a Middle-Class Society

Even though the Second Aliyah had brought the future political elite to Palestine by the eve of the First
World War and had laid the ideological foundations for
interwar society, it was not until the postwar immigration that the numerical foundation for the development
of independent statehood was established. The altered
circumstances of a British-ruled Palestine, and the fact
that living conditions in the Jewish Diaspora in Eastern
Europe had dramatically worsened following the ap-
palling pogroms in the Ukraine in 1919–20 and the rise
of political antisemitism in central Europe, contributed
to a sharp rise in the number of Jewish immigrants.

The approximately 35,000 immigrants of the Third
Aliyah (1919–23) were still strongly motivated by the
ideology of the workers' movement. Many of them had
already been trained in agriculture in Europe as prescribed by the Hehaluz ("pioneer") movement, and they
invigorated the kibbutz system in Palestine. Altogether
different circumstances prevailed during the Fourth
Aliyah, which started in the mid-1920s. New American
laws of 1921 and 1924 had resulted in significant restrictions on immigration in the country that had previously taken in the majority of the Jewish refugees from
Eastern Europe. Moreover, emigration from the Soviet
Union, the source of most of the socialist-minded immigrants, had become far more difficult. Immigrants
during the second half of the 1920s were mostly from

Poland and primarily middle-class. They constituted the basis of the urban middle classes of Palestine, reinforced during the Fifth Aliyah in the 1930s by refugees from Nazi-dominated Europe. In 1936, the Jewish population reached nearly 400,000 and constituted almost one-third of the total population of Palestine.

The Zionist worker's movement had succeeded over the course of years in transforming the Jewish population of Palestine from a passive recipient of assistance from the outside to an active force that set its own destiny. The agricultural settlements were vital to the ideology of this transformation, since they represented the physical regeneration of the Jews that had been called for since the Enlightenment. Nonetheless, over 90 percent of the Jews who lived in Palestine after the First World War resided in the cities, which in many cases were newly created.

Tel Aviv, founded in 1909 north of Jaffa, was of par-

The much disputed "kiosk," a first sign of urbanization, built one year after the founding of Tel Aviv, in 1910.

ticular significance. The foundation of the "first Jewish
city" gave rise to numerous legends. According to one
legend, the first sixty plots were distributed by lottery
among the founders of the city. Another one claimed
that the first sandy paths were built upwards from the
beach and led to a "kiosk," which was the first mark of
urbanization. According to a third legend, it took only a
few years for an infrastructure with shops and schools to
develop. Many writers incorporated this development
into their literary writings, notably Shmuel Yosef Agnon
in *T'mol Shilshom* (Yesterday and the Day Before) and
Samuel Yshar, whose novel *Mikdamot* (Preludes) portrayed the first streets of Tel Aviv, the transformation
from an agricultural cooperative to an urban middle-
class life and the violent riots of 1921.

The immigration movement from Poland that com-
menced in 1924 and the influx from the German-speaking countries that followed a few years later had a crucial impact on Tel Aviv. Within a few years, Tel Aviv had
evolved from a garden suburb of Jaffa to a lively Mediterranean metropolis with cafés and elegant shops. Its
population rose from 2,000 in 1914 to 34,000 one decade later; by 1935 it had reached 120,000. A visitor
touring the city in the 1920s could not help noting sim-
ilarities to America even that far back: "A vigorously
alive, a boundlessly ambitious town was Tel-Aviv in the
days of its breathless onward rushes, nursing all sorts
of American aspirations, straining after such distant
models as Atlantic City and Miami..."[46] Visible evidence

of this modernization was the architecture of the city, which was strongly influenced by the Bauhaus style and had whimsical villas that featured biblical, modern, European, or Chinese motifs.

In 1923, the newspaper *Ha'aretz* moved from Jerusalem to Tel Aviv, and in 1925 competition arrived in the form of the influential daily *Davar*, which was published by the Histadrut. The Ohel Theater was established in the same year as a major cultural institution. The Philharmonic Orchestra and the Tel Aviv Museum followed in the 1930s. The Habima Theater, which was founded in Moscow and became internationally renowned in the course of many tours, would now become permanently established in Tel Aviv. The most famous Hebrew writers, Ahad Ha'am and Chaim Nachman Bialik, settled there as well. The 1920s and 1930s were a decisive phase in the development of other cities, especially of Haifa in the north.

Many other plans went awry. Sometimes their failures were metaphorical, such as the grandiose plans of the architect Richard Kaufmann, who wanted to build on his success with garden suburbs in various areas by constructing a new metropolis complete with opera and other cultural institutions in Afula. At other times, however, the collapse was quite literal. The Casino on the beach in Tel Aviv, which looked like a big circus tent, was not a gambling casino as its name would indicate, but the most popular café in the city—until it disintegrated in the waves of the Mediterranean.

Foundational Myths

The establishment of a Jewish society in Palestine, both in agricultural settlements and in cities, proceeded at a swift pace and probably would have been unstoppable had the land really been as empty as many early Zionists had imagined. Samuel Yshar gave literary expression to this notion, which was prevalent among people poised to emigrate to Palestine in Eastern Europe, in his novel *Mikdamot* (Preludes): "Who knew anything about Arabs? No one had ever mentioned them. In all of those speeches, lectures, and debates in the Volhynian forests at the banks of the Styr, which flowed along lazily in the comfortable carefree twilight and with almost apathetic tranquillity listened to the boldest songs of home and the most conclusive evidence that we would only find a home in our own land, they, the Arabs, never came up, not in any discussion or other deliberations, and most assuredly not in the songs; they simply did not exist."[47]

The fact that Arabs really did exist was immediately apparent to the immigrants upon their arrival. They would also soon learn that they were not as welcome as Herzl had imagined in his novel *Old New Land*. At least some part of the Arab population of Palestine would turn against these new neighbors, whom they considered foreign intruders. The first riots against the immigrants came in 1881. The immigrants, who had just fled the pogroms in Russia, interpreted these disturbances in

Yemenite Jew serving as a guardsman in a postcard from Warsaw around 1910.

the spirit of the events they were accustomed to from the Old World, namely as a recurrence of the pogroms in the Orient. Their reactions, of course, were different. In contrast to the stereotype of physically weak and defenseless Jews in exile who were at the mercy of antisemitic violence, Zionists in Palestine projected an image of readiness to defend themselves to the death. Thus, the ideal of the Jewish sentry joined the twin ideals of the Jewish farmer and worker.

One of the first written testimonies of the new Jewish myth of resistance was *Yiskor* ("Commemorate"), a book published in 1911 with the telling subtitle: "A Book Commemorating Guardsmen Killed in Action and Workers in the Land of Israel." Martin Buber contributed a preface to the 1918 German edition, which was (anonymously) translated by Gershom Scholem. He began with three key words of the new way of life in

Palestine: "Settle—Work—Watch. These three watch-
words encompass the exterior and interior history of the
developing new community of people in this land."[48]

In his introduction, the young David Ben-Gurion
used the example of the model settlement of Sejera to
demonstrate the necessity of posting Jewish guards in
the settlements threatened by attacks. Just as Jewish
laborers were replacing foreign workers, agricultural
colonies would have to employ their own guards. The
need for the immigrants from the Diaspora to take their
fate into their own hands and not depend on others is
clearly evident here. As understandable as this way
of thinking was after centuries of minority status in
Europe, it virtually guaranteed conflict with the Arabs,
who feared the loss of their jobs.

Just a few years after this book was published, a highly symbolic incident occurred in the Tel Hai settlement
on the northern border of Palestine. In March 1920,
eight Jewish settlers lost their lives during an attack by
Arabs. One of them was Joseph Trumpeldor (1880–
1920), a former officer in the Russian army who had lost
an arm in the Russo-Japanese War. During the World
War, he had attempted to establish a Jewish unit in the
Russian army. When he immigrated to Palestine in
1912, he already enjoyed hero status, which assumed
mythic dimensions after his death. He was considered
the shining example of the pioneer who despite his emi-
nence in the Diaspora would go to great lengths to build
up his own national homeland. His last words ("It is

good to die for our country") served as the basis for poems, songs, and legends about his life. On the graves of the eight men who died at Tel Hai, which serves as a site of pilgrimage, the following message is inscribed: "In blood and fire Judaea fell; in blood and fire Judaea will rise." The saying comes from a poem by Ya'akov Cahan (1881–1960), who gave lyric expression to the need for a new Jewish spirit of heroism. The opening lines of his poem "Ha-Biryonim" (the name of a violent group of Jewish insurgents against the Romans; in modern Hebrew it would translate as "The Ruffians") is equally dramatic:

> We have been resurrected, we have returned, the Biryonim
> We came to save our oppressed land
> With a strong hand we demand our rights!

Just as Trumpeldor had become the epitome of modern heroism in Zionism, the status of ancient heroes was now enhanced as well. Two thousand years earlier, these heroes had been regarded as paragons of Jewish self-sacrifice for their national cause: the Maccabees, who took back and purified the temple in Jerusalem that had been desecrated by the Greeks in the second century B.C.E., and Bar Kokhba, who died a martyr in the second century C.E. as a rebel against the Roman occupation. Even though Bar Kokhba was a political failure and hardly a role model in the rabbinical literature through the centuries, the Zionists contended that he had demonstrated dignity and self-esteem in his struggle against the occupiers of the homeland. These qualities were of prime significance in the Hebrew literature of those years. The mass suicide at Masada in 73 C.E. was now regarded as an act of heroic resistance to the powerful Romans by the last Jewish bastion.

The quest for heroes and collective myths is common to all incipient national movements. In the case of Zionism, it was part of a process, along with producing a modern Hebrew lexicon, compiling a Jewish encyclopedia, and defining "Jewish" art and music, that historians today call "invention of tradition." Especially alluring in the case of Zionism was the opportunity for those who lived far away from Zion to contribute to building a modern Jewish nation by means of cultural engagement, donations to the Jewish National Fund, and identification with the new Zionist ideals.

In the case of the Jewish nation, it would be more appropriate to use the phrase "reinvention of tradition," because in contrast to many other nations, the roots of its own statehood did exist, but had been submerged for a long period of time. Thus, the Zionist understanding of history that began to develop in the early 20th century is a logical consequence of this "reinvention," which was based on an extremely selective view of history. It cuts out much of medieval Jewish history of the Diaspora or portrays it in a negative light. "Actual" Jewish history unfolded in the period of political sovereignty before the destruction of the Second Temple in 70 C.E. and became significant once again when Zionism began in the 19th century.

Zionism defines itself in terms of ancient times and therefore downgrades the period of the centuries in exile, which were thought to be almost devoid of history. What is more, Zionism regards itself as a revolution against its own history. In any case, this is how the future Israeli Prime Minister David Ben-Gurion characterized it in an emotional address to a group of Zionist youth leaders in Haifa in 1944: "Our revolution is directed not only against a system but against *destiny*, against the unique destiny of a unique people."[49] Before the backdrop of the genocide in Europe, Ben-Gurion described the two thousand years of Jewish existence in exile as a history of persecution and assimilation. Now the time had come, he explained, to put an end once and for all to Diaspora existence: "Galut means dependence—material, political, spiritual, cultural, and intellectual dependence—because we are aliens, a minority, bereft of a homeland, rootless and separated from the soil, from labor, and from basic industry. Our task is to break radically with this dependence and to become masters of our own fate—in a word, to achieve independence."[50]

The ideal of the "new Jew," a term also adopted by Zionist sports clubs, drew on ancient heroes. Their names were Maccabee, Bar Kokhba, Betar (the name of Bar Kokhba's final place of refuge), or simply Hakoah ("strength"). The fact that Hakoah Wien became the

JÜDISCHE TURNERSCHAFT
II. KREIS WESTOESTERREICH

Jewish gymnast depicting the new ideal of the "muscle Jew" in a Viennese postcard around the turn of the century.

Austrian soccer champion in the 1920s may have been a more momentous political achievement for Zionism than many political resolutions of that period. Equally important was the Zionist youth movement, which split into every political direction from socialist to mainstream and religious and comprised a substantial proportion of the young generation. Here, too, ancient symbols of Jewish heroism often had an important role, as is evident from the name "Betar," adopted by the Revisionist youth movement, and the Prague Zionist association's name "Bar Kokhba."

Elaborate legends soon grew up around the Maccabees, Bar Kokhba, Masada, and Tel Hai. Sites of pilgrimage were erected and songs were composed. The festival of Hanukkah, which was associated with the Maccabees, assumed a new significance with the rise of Zionism that had not been accorded it in traditional Judaism. An important factor was certainly the proximity of this holiday to Christmas; its enhanced value could therefore also be welcomed by assimilated Jews who sought a counterpart to the most important Christian holiday. The defeat of Bar Kokhba and the victims at Masada served as an ongoing reminder of outside dangers. The necessity of putting up a fight was often justified by these historical examples. After the foundation of the State of Israel, David Ben-Gurion pointed out that modern soldiers maintained an historical continuity with the heroism of the ancients: "The chain that was broken in the days of Shimon Bar Kokhba and Akiba ben Yosef was reinforced in our days, and the Israeli army is again ready for the battle in its own land, to fight for the freedom of the nation and the homeland."[51]

One of the best-known Israeli rituals is the traditional swearing-in ceremony for soldiers on Masada under the motto: "Masada shall never fall again!" The fact that archeology has enjoyed a special significance in the State of Israel, and that prominent politicians such as Moshe Dayan and Yigael Yadin did archeological work, directly reflects the high value placed on ancient hero myths.

The image of "sabras," Jews born in the country who have a rough skin, work the soil with their own hands, and defend themselves bearing weapons, also originated in opposition to the aesthetic and defenseless Jew in exile. However, it would be wrong to assume that resistance to mythologizing Jewish history and applying it to the relations with Arabs in Palestine started with the recent debates at the close of the 20th century. These debates are as old as Zionism itself.

Some of the early Hebrew writers also provided perceptive descriptions of their situation in relation to the Palestinian population. One of the most distinguished of these writers, Yosef Chaim Brenner, wrote after a bloody Arab attack on Jewish settlers: "The murderer is a resident of this land, his language is the language of the land . . . By contrast, the victim is a foreigner here."[52] Unlike Ya'akov Cahan, who admired the *Biryonim* and drew a sharp distinction between existence in the Diaspora and in Israel, Brenner applied the classic Diaspora terms "victim" and "foreign" to the Jews of Palestine as well. In his novel *Mi-kan u-mi-kan* ("From Here and There," 1911), from which the above sentences are taken, he even went so far as to write: "It turns out that there is no difference . . . Exile is everywhere . . . Are we safe here? The angel of death has his eyes everywhere."[53] Still more tragic was the fact that Brenner's open doubts whether Palestine was really the requisite asylum for persecuted Jews would be confirmed on his own body. He was one of the 95 casualties of the riots in May 1921, the worst clashes between Jews and Arabs in Jaffa to date. These were preceded by demonstrations of socialist and communist Jews in Tel Aviv and Jaffa on the occasion of May Day, which was the trigger for some Arabs to storm an immigrants' hostel in Jaffa and cause a bloodbath there. The May riots brought about a split of Tel Aviv from Jaffa, and many Jews moved to the

"Jewish" city.

Although Trumpeldor's attempt to establish a Jewish unit in the Russian army was thwarted by the Russian withdrawal from the war, Vladimir Jabotinsky was able to set up a Jewish legion with the British army toward the end of the war. However, this legion had a purely symbolic significance in the quest for a national homeland. It expressed the need for a Jewish army for the first time in the modern era. For most Zionists, a Jewish army was just as important as a symbol of their own independent statehood as speaking their own language, working the soil, and establishing a modern Hebrew culture.

However, there were dissenting voices here too, vociferously protesting against "blood and fire" slogans and the formation of a Jewish legion. A.D. Gordon was unsparing in his criticism. He considered the army a non-Jewish institution. Even Herzl had not provided any place of honor for a Jewish army. To the extent that it was necessary at all, it would fulfill more or less the role of auxiliary police. Gordon went much further. The military and militarism, he claimed, had never helped any people to survive. What kept nations alive was the power of their great ideals, including the ideal behind the saying "Nation shall not lift sword against nation." In stark contrast to the voices cited above, Gordon spoke out against "those who see in the deeds of the fist lofty heroism."[54] Gordon considered the army "the blind, elemental force of the people . . . a remnant of the period

when the nation, animal-like, beast-like, did not yet
know how to define its individuality, how to assert its
relationship to the other tribes except by beating, push-
ing, biting."[55] In the contrasting positions of Gordon
and Jabotinsky and the many shades between them, the
enormous points of friction in Zionist policy were already taking shape. By the end of World War I at the lat-
est it was hardly possible to speak of one single Zionism.
There were many Zionisms, often diametrically opposed
on fundamental questions, though united in their basic
claim to a Jewish home in Palestine.

CHAPTER FOUR

One Zionism or Many Zionisms? The Formation of Zionist Parties

A poster of the Revisionist party demands the opening of the doors for free immigration to Palestine in the period of the British Mandate. The map in the background shows Greater Eretz Israel including Jordan.

Even during Herzl's lifetime, differences within Zionism had emerged, but the conflicts were played out between individuals and not by means of parties. The delegates to the first Zionist Congresses, which took place annually at first and every second year from 1903 on, were not sent by political parties, but by national associations organized by territory. They regarded themselves as "General Zionists," whose ideological allegiance was solely to a vaguely defined Zionism. All of the Presidents of the "Zionist Organization" after Theodor Herzl considered themselves part of this tradition: David Wolffsohn (President, 1905–11), Otto Warburg (1911–20), Chaim Weizmann (1920–31 and 1935–46), and Nahum Sokolow (1931–35).

The Beginnings of Factionalism

The first instance of infighting at a Zionist Congress appeared when the Democratic Faction came on the scene in 1901. A group of young intellectuals, influenced by the cultural Zionism of Ahad Ha'am, among them Chaim Weizmann, Leo Motzkin, and Martin Buber, presented their own positions. The goals of this group went beyond the primary task of establishing a homeland safe from persecution and sought to create a new secular Jewish culture in the Hebrew language. The major demands of this faction included establishing a Hebrew university in Jerusalem, a publishing house for

In this drawing by Ephraim Moses Lilien, an angel shows the stooped Ghetto Jew the thorny way to the upright Jewish farmer's life. Lilien's "Jugendstil" (art deco) drawings, prints, and photographs helped shape the public's early image of Zionism.

Zionist publications, and a new national Jewish art. The latter's main representative was the Jugendstil artist Moses Ephraim Lilien, himself a member of the Democratic Faction. His drawings, prints, and photographs created a Zionist iconography and substantially shaped the public image of Zionism.

The Democratic Faction was not directed primarily at Herzl, but at the religious delegates who skirted any cultural issues at the Zionist Congresses. Most Orthodox Jews opposed political Zionism right from the start despite their traditionally strong allegiance to the idea of Zion. Although religious Jews pray for a return to Zion three times a day, this return must be initiated by

God as part of a religious redemption in the messianic realm. However, when assimilated Jews like Herzl and Nordau founded a secular political movement before the coming of the Messiah, this movement could only be interpreted as blasphemous.

Of course a minority thought otherwise and joined the tradition of a religious Zionism that had been created by rabbis, notably Yehuda Alkalai and Zvi Hirsch Kalischer. In their view, the settlement of the Holy Land and the goals of political Zionism accorded with tradition and were even desirable. The messianic dimension of the return to Zion was marginalized by these religious Zionists. They felt that the predominantly secular Zionist Organization ought to steer clear of questions concerning culture and education. When the Democratic Faction was founded at the Fifth Zionist Congress and took up the cause of precisely these objectives, an organizational merger of the religious Zionists was provoked in 1902. Under the leadership of Rabbi Isaac Jacob Reines (1839–1915), they were known as Mizrachi, which was an acronym for "spiritual center," but also meant "eastward."

In Russia, a further political orientation, socialist Zionism, developed within the Zionist movement, and set the tone for Zionism after World War I. The early theorists of this movement, Nachman Syrkin (1868–1924), Ber Borochov (1881–1917), and Berl Katznelson (1877–1944), tried out various ways of bringing the social question into line with the territorial question.

Common to both issues was a desire to recast the Jews as workers and farmers rather than as merchants and to promote a gradual flow of emigration from the Diaspora to their own state. Elimination of capitalism and putting an end to the political impotence of the Jews went hand in hand.

As was common in the left camp, several competing parties were formed right from the start. In the view of the Marxist-oriented Poalei Zion ("workers of Zion"), antisemitism stemmed from the anomalous economic situation of the Jews. In their own state they would be economically regenerated and ultimately constitute one normal socialist nation among others in the course of the international socialist revolution. The Poalei Zion viewed itself as a Jewish national branch of the world revolution. Hapoel Hatzair ("The Young Worker") was less ideological. Although its members also used socialist categories, the priority of this group remained Jewish nationalism. It stressed the unique quality of the Jewish nation, which first had to conquer its own territory, and focused on the pragmatic task of making the Jews productive in the land of Israel (the "conquest of labor") over all other party goals. The left faction of the Poalei Zion and the Hashomer Hatzair ("The Young Watchman"), affiliated with the kibbutz movement, remained active as separate parties within Zionism. The two main Zionist parties, Ahdut Ha'Avoda and Hapoel Hatzair, merged in 1930 to form the Palestinian Labor Party. Two smaller groups, however, the Poalei Zion and the

Hashomer Hatzair, did not join. Several Russian members of the left-wing Poalei Zion had cast their lot with the Communists. For many decades, the socialist direction would dominate the Zionist Organization and later the State of Israel, but was unsuccessful in forming a truly unified party out of the diverse ideological camps.

Revisionism came on the scene as a final major ideological direction within Zionism. It represented middle-class, antisocialist, and nationalist elements within the movement. The dominant figure of Revisionism was Vladimir Ze'ev Jabotinsky (1880–1940), one of the most dazzling presences in Jewish politics in the first half of the 20th century. He had made a name for himself in the literary world of Russia as a journalist, writer, and translator. His brilliance as an orator soon secured him a large following, the primary basis of which was the mainstream middle class of Polish Jewry of the interwar period. Jabotinsky considered himself the true successor of Herzl, whom he admired greatly, and he initially tried to influence the Zionist movement from within. Like Herzl, he gave higher priority to political and diplomatic efforts than to cultural goals. He also emphasized the necessity of military battle and was successful in establishing a Jewish Legion in the British army during the First World War. The youth organization Betar also had the character of a paramilitary group. It was not until 1925 that Jabotinsky created his own Revisionist party. Ten years later, he and his party left the Zionist Organization because of its allegedly conciliatory line toward the British and Arabs, and Jabotinsky founded his own "New Zionist Organization."

These four political camps—General Zionists or liberals, religious groups, socialists, and Revisionists—have continued to cover the spectrum of the political landscape of the State of Israel, and consist of many small factions even today. In contrast to the political idyll that Theodor Herzl depicted in *Old New Land*, these various groups were often fiercely embattled. Their visions of a Jewish state parted ways when it came to four fundamental questions: What behavior is appropriate toward the Arab population? Which path should be taken to achieve state sovereignty? What role should religion play in the Jewish state? On what type of economic order is the Jewish state based?

Jews and Arabs

Theodor Herzl found his own solution to the problem of confrontation with the Arab population by deciding that the issue simply did not exist. The only Arab protagonist in his novel *Old New Land*, Reschid Bey, welcomes the European immigrants and considers them a blessing. Orange exports increase tenfold after their arrival, the Arabs experience the pleasures of the fruits of European civilization, and in this Switzerland of the Middle East, constructed by the Jews, they also learn European ways. Herzl takes it for granted that nothing better could happen to them. The actual interests of the Arab population have virtually no role in Herzl's scheme of things.

Not all early Zionists were as naive in this regard. Herzl's critic Ahad Ha'am pointed out from the start that the Jewish immigrants would not be welcomed with open arms by the Arab population. Ahad Ha'am's fears were borne out right away. As early as 1891, a group of influential Arabs from Jerusalem protested against Jewish immigration and the ensuing purchases of land in an official letter to Istanbul. Although the immigration that was advocated by the Zionists proceeded at a very slow pace, contemporaries at the turn of the century reported numerous clashes between the immigrants and the indigenous population. The Arab national movement was suppressed as long as the Sultan in the region could rule absolutely. With the Young Turk revolution of 1908, a political turning point was introduced in the Middle East. A newly founded Arab press propounded a new nationalism, against which Zionism now represented a major adversary in the struggle for Arab independence.

Socialist Zionist attitudes toward the Arab population were riddled with contradictions. They regarded the Arabs as a populace that was just as economically exploited and politically disadvantaged as they themselves and could be potential allies in the struggle against the world powers of the Russian Tsar and the Ottoman Sultan. However, they were well aware that their claim to national sovereignty in Palestine precluded similar demands on the Arab side. Although they considered all people equal, they viewed the dissemination of western ideas and technological progress in the Marxist sense as an absolute requirement for a successful class struggle. Despite their declared belief in pacifism, they led an armed defense after indigenous Arab villagers attacked the new settlers. Their experience of defenselessness in the face of pogroms in Tsarist Russia undoubtedly played a psychological role in motivating their actions. Ultimately their notion of "conquest by labor," which was designed to turn Jews into farmers and workers, left them no choice but gradually to displace local residents from particular areas and professions despite any theoretical esteem they might have for the Arabs.

Thus, a deep rift developed between the socialist Zionists' theoretical claim to see the Arabs as their cousins (if not as their brothers) facing a common foe, and their daily reality: Their Jewish socialist striving for independence, their western sense of mission, their notion of self-defense, and their concept of agricultural work met with very different ideas in the Arab population. David Ben-Gurion's claim at a party conference in 1924 that the rights of the Arab population to the land in Palestine could not be recognized because they had not worked the land could hardly evoke sympathy from the Arabs. Ben-Gurion argued that anyone who left the land fallow and neglected it forfeited his claim to it. Khalil al-Sakakini, an influential Arab living in Jerusalem, captured the sentiment of his fellow countrymen toward Ben-Gurion in an article in the Arab newspaper *Falastin* with this sarcastic greeting: "Welcome, cousins! We are the guests and you are the masters of the house."[56]

Ben-Gurion validated the historical claim of the Jews to the land of their origins as well as their responsibility for it. However, the basic idea that the workers and farmers on the Jewish and the Arab sides would ultimately work together and were natural allies continued to inform the official position of the socialist Zionists for a long time to come.

The General Zionists, by contrast, tried to solve the arising national conflict by means of *realpolitik*. Herzl and his successors before the First World War made diplomacy the priority of Zionist politics. Only on the basis of Jewish sovereignty could the Arabs be granted anything. Achieving sovereignty was therefore the first goal they pursued. After World War I, it really began to look as if a consensual solution could be attained by means of diplomacy. In order to secure supremacy in the region, the British made concessions to both the Jews and the Arabs during the war, which could be kept only if Jews and Arabs acknowledged each others' rights.

In January 1919, Chaim Weizmann, who emerged from the war as the leading figure of the Zionists, signed an agreement with the son of the sharif Husayn of Mecca, the emir Feisal, in which the Arabs recognized Jewish claims to Palestine. In this agreement, both sides affirmed: "All necessary measures shall be taken to encourage and stimulate the immigration of Jews into Palestine on a large scale, and as quickly as possible to settle Jewish immigrants upon the land through closer settlement and intensive cultivation of the soil. In taking such measures the Arab peasant and tenant farmers shall be protected in their rights, and shall be assisted in forwarding their economic development."[57] However, a postscript to the agreement stated that the agreement would be valid only if Arab independence were to be established, as stipulated elsewhere by Feisal. Still, Feisal assured a leading American Zionist, Felix Frankfurter, in response to his inquiries: "We Arabs, especially the educated among us, look with the deepest sympathy on the Zionist movement; . . . we will wish the Jews a most hearty welcome home . . . We are working together for a reformed and revived Near East, and our two movements complete one another . . . Indeed I think that neither can be a real success without the other."[58] Feisal's vision of a greater Arab empire led by him ultimately ran counter to the plans of the colonial powers, and he later claimed not to recall this letter, which was dismissed as a Zionist forgery by the Arab side. His real motive for signing it may have been to win over the British as patrons during the Paris Peace Conference, or simply Feisal's scanty interest in Palestine, since he was focused on Syria. In any case, it would have been virtually impossible to persuade the Arab population to cede sovereignty over Palestine at that time. Any agreement based solely on diplomacy in the absence of reconciliation between the two peoples was doomed to failure.

Nevertheless, documents like these inspired the leading Zionists, both liberal and socialist, to believe that reconciliation with the Arab population was within reach. Chaim Weizmann commented on Feisal's letter as follows: "This remarkable letter should be of interest to the critics who have accused us of beginning our Zionist work in Palestine without ever consulting the wishes or welfare of the Arab world. It must be borne in mind that the views here expressed by the then acknowledged leader of the Arabs, the bearer of their hopes, were the culmination of several discussions."[59] After World War I, leading British politicians remained confident, in a manner that recalled Herzl, that the Palestinian Arabs would welcome the Europeans as long as they brought them the fruits of civilization.

The Revisionist position differed altogether from that of the Socialist and the General Zionists. The Revisionists were also political realists, but their brand of realism did not mesh with that of the official Zionist leadership. Their design featured a Jewish state on both sides of the Jordan. If the Arab people adapted to this state, they could remain; otherwise they would need to resettle in Arab states. Only from a position of strength could the Jews approach the Arabs, who were regarded as foes, not as allies, right from the outset. Jabotinsky had great respect for the Arab position, but he considered his own claim morally legitimated by the greater threat facing

the Jews in Europe. He regarded Herzl's assumption that
the founding of a state could proceed bloodlessly and
the immigrants would be welcomed in friendship by the
Arabs as an illusion. Of course Herzl had grown up in
a tradition of European liberalism, and his concept of a
Jewish state was predicated on the principle of the
equality of all residents of any faith or nationality.

Diverse Paths to the Jewish State

When Herzl first spoke of a Jewish state, it was not
clear, nor had it been earlier for Pinsker, whether he
meant Palestine, Argentina, or some other autonomous
territory. In 1903, one year before his death, he considered reviewing a British proposal to found a Jewish settlement in East Africa. The so-called Uganda Project (the
area was actually located in what is now Kenya) would
split apart Zionism more than any previous issue. It was
clear to Herzl that Uganda could not replace Zion and
offered nothing but a "night shelter," as Max Nordau
called it. The project was eventually abandoned, but
even this brief look away from Zion made many Zionists
think of Herzl as a traitor. A small minority of Zionists
who did not regard Zion as the exclusive locus of the
realization of Jewish statehood left the movement after
Herzl's death and founded the Jewish Territorial Organization (ITO) under the leadership of the Anglo-Jewish
writer Israel Zangwill in 1905. This organization advo-

cated land purchases in Australia and other parts of the world, but it soon faded into oblivion.

The deep connection felt by both non-religious and religious Zionists to the soil of Palestine was so strong that any other geographical option was ultimately doomed to failure. The relationship to the land of their forefathers, which was maintained through the centuries with prayers and poems, language and imagination, made Zionists across the spectrum cling to the territorial claim of the Jews to Palestine. The General Zionists from Herzl to Weizmann typically avoided religious arguments and stressed instead their "historic right" to Eretz Israel, the land of Israel. Socialist Zionists did not maintain that their people had a claim to a specific territory legitimated by history, but for most of them any alternative was ruled out for pragmatic reasons, since only Palestine was sufficiently appealing to the Jewish masses and at the same time open to emigration and the establishment of a new society.

The position of Jabotinsky and the Revisionists deviated less in theory than in practice. Jabotinsky was quick to realize that two peoples had legitimate claims to the same country. In contrast to the socialists, who preached reserve and compromise with the Arabs, he saw armed conflict as the only solution. The Arabs would refuse to agree to a Jewish state, as Jabotinsky well understood. His moral argument to justify the precedence of the Jewish claims was based on the political reality of the situation. While the Arabs already had numerous states, the Jews were fighting for one single state, which they urgently and promptly needed in view of the persecutions they were facing. Characteristic of Jabotinsky's argumentation was his speech to the Palestine Royal Commission in 1937, against the backdrop of antisemitic persecutions in Europe. He claimed to have understood fully that the Palestinian Arabs in Palestine wanted to found a fourth or fifth or sixth Arab state: "but when the Arab claim is confronted with our Jewish demand to be saved, it is like the claims of appetite versus the claims of starvation."[60]

Only in the national-religious camp and among a small group of liberal intellectuals were there radically different concepts of the claim to Eretz Israel and the consequent political visions. The national-religious movement of Mizrachi was the only one to uphold the Jews' claim to the land of Israel on religious rather than on historical or political grounds, citing the Bible, from the time of God's covenant with Abraham, in which he promised the land of Canaan to Abraham's descendants, as the source of the legitimacy of unbroken Jewish claims to the Holy Land. Questions concerning what borders would have to be drawn in the Holy Land and what position the Arab population would hold would have aroused heated controversy even within the national-religious camp. However, the God-given claim of the Jews to return to their land was in their eyes incontestable from the outset.

The philosopher Martin Buber (1878–1965) certainly

believed that Zionism would fulfill a religious mission, but he was not at all convinced that the Jews had any historical right to this land, which made him an exception among the Zionists. If each chapter of world history is preceded by another, he argued, then surely the peoples who had lived in Palestine *before* the Israelites would have an even greater historical claim to it. The claim of the Arabs, who had once conquered the land, was of course not greater than that of the Jews, who had been driven out of it. The land had room enough for both peoples. Buber supported the idea of a binational state, which the Brit Shalom (Covenant of Peace) was attempting to achieve. This organization existed for only a brief period (1925–33). The groups that succeeded it were few in number. Their members were respected intellectuals who typically came from Central Europe. However, they lacked counterparts on the Arab side who recognized a Jewish right to a home in Palestine.

During the first few decades of Zionist politics, the issue of how to approach the Arabs stood in the shadow of diplomatic efforts to solicit the support of the world powers. Herzl was eagerly seeking audiences with the Pope and the Sultan, the German Kaiser and Russian ministers. Although he did not achieve many concrete outcomes in the process, his persistence brought Zionism onto the international political arena. Chaim Weizmann would reap the benefits of the priority of diplomacy set by the General Zionists during the First World War. His good relations with the British govern-

ment enabled him to wrest a pledge from a pivotal power
to establish a Jewish national home for the first time.

The Balfour Declaration of November 2, 1917 represented a decisive diplomatic breakthrough for Zionism,
and until the 1940s was the most significant official document to which its leading representatives could refer. In
just a few short lines, the British Foreign Secretary A. J.
Balfour had assured Lord Rothschild with the explicit
agreement of the cabinet that the government of His
Majesty was favorably inclined to the establishment of a
national home of the Jewish people in Palestine and
would facilitate the realization of this goal. Since this
declaration would encounter substantial resistance from
the British Jewish establishment, Balfour also gave his
assurance that the rights and status of Jews who remained in the Diaspora would not be violated. The crucial phrase in the document, stating that the royal government "views with favour the establishment in Palestine of a national home for the Jewish people," was equi-
vocal. "In Palestine" could mean all of Palestine or only
a small portion of it; "national home" was not a legally
defined term, and "views with favour" was certainly not
a contractual guarantee on the part of England. In spite
of his disappointment about this ambiguity, Weizmann
was keenly aware that he was holding in his hands the
first written document that could be presented to the
world at large. Weizmann was firmly convinced that the
Jewish state could only be established by means of good
relations with Britain. Thus, Zionist politics of the 1920s

and 1930s were marked by Weizmann's firm commitment to the mandatory power despite any setbacks.

Jabotinsky was also initially an ally and admirer of the British. After all, he had been able to establish a Jewish Legion within the British army during the First World War. However, the differences between his position and Weizmann's were already evident here. Jabotinsky placed greater emphasis on the military side, hence the paramilitary character of the Revisionist youth organization Betar. Without a doubt, Jabotinsky respected Weizmann's diplomatic efforts and Ahad Ha'am's cultural initiatives, but in order to achieve his maximalist call for a Jewish state on both sides of the Jordan, he first had to establish a concrete reality. Immigration took precedence over all of his other goals. According to his own calculations, 40,000 Jews would need to emigrate to Palestine per year over the course of 25 years in order to achieve a Jewish majority at the earliest possible date.

The Revisionists had been taking an increasingly critical position toward Britain since the mid-1930s. This criticism mellowed of necessity during their common battle against Nazi Germany in the war years, but afterwards it was merged into terrorist violence.

The Role of Religion

Clashes on religious issues were relatively inconsequential in the early phase of the Zionist movement. This is hardly surprising, since most Orthodox Jews distanced themselves from Zionism, and the great majority of the Zionists in turn viewed themselves as part of a secular movement. All of their other differences notwithstanding, this outlook applied equally to Herzl, Ahad Ha'am, Weizmann, Jabotinsky, and Ben-Gurion. All of them saw Zionism not only as a means for the Jews to return to their ancestral home and their rescue from physical distress in Europe, but also as a unique opportunity to construct a new secular Jewish identity.

Herzl, Nordau, and other Central European Zionists had already called for a "new Jew" at the turn of the century. Max Nordau's catchy term *Muskeljude* ("muscular Jew") inspired the establishment of Jewish gymnastics clubs. Herzl promulgated a new Jewish aesthetics as exemplified in the art of Ephraim Moses Lilien. The impelling force for a physical and cultural transformation of everything that could be identified as Jewish, however, came from Eastern Europe. Ahad Ha'am was a pivotal figure in this quest for transformation. The more radical Hebrew-language writers, such as Saul Tchernichowsky (1875–1943), who used pagan Greek antiquity as a model, Micha Yosef Berdichevsky (also called Bin-Gorion, 1865–1921), who was influenced by Nietzsche's call for a transvaluation of all values, and Yosef Chaim

Brenner (1881–1921), who insisted on liberation from any type of religion, made a complete break with Jewish tradition, and attempted to create a new secular self-awareness for the Jewish people. Ultimately very little of this radical thinking remained in the Jewish society of Palestine, aside from the movement of the Canaanites, who were led by Jonathan Ratosh (whose real name was Uriel Halperin, 1908–81) and during the 1940s and 1950s boasted considerable influence. Their major area of concern was the complete separation of Jews living in Palestine from the fate of the Diaspora Jews while simultaneously integrating them into the culture of the Middle East. The Jews became Hebrews, whose history and destiny were linked to their immediate surroundings and not to the two thousand years of dispersion. For these thinkers, religion functioned solely as an antagonist.

The national-religious Mizrachi movement took the opposite position within Zionism. It did not call for the establishment of a religious state in which Jewish religious law, the *halakhah*, would become the law of the land, but was primarily concerned with keeping issues of education and culture out of the official discussions of the Zionist Congress as far as possible and creating legitimate islands within a nonreligious or even antireligious society. It did not aspire to a religious state, but a state in which religious people as well as non-religious people could choose their own way of life.

Rabbi Reines, the founder of Mizrachi, was a political

Zionist in the Herzlian sense, concerned with alleviating
the physical suffering of the Jews. He argued that in this
regard it was irrelevant whether Zionists were religious
or non-religious. In contrast to most of his orthodox
contemporaries, he did not consider Zionism a blasphemous movement that took into its own hands what
ought to be reserved for the age of the Messiah. However, unlike many of his successors, he did not regard it
as a movement that would help usher in the Messianic
age. Reines and the early religious Zionists were more
apt to marginalize the messianic element and could
thus bring religious orthodoxy and national ideology
into accord.

This would remain the dominant ideology in the
national-religious movement for a long time to come,
although a new way of thinking began to hold sway
in the 1920s with the growing influence of the first
Ashkenazic chief rabbi of Palestine and arguably the
foremost Jewish mystic of his generation, Avraham Yitzhak Ha-Cohen Kook (1865–1937; chief rabbi from 1921
to 1935). For Rabbi Kook, Zionism was significant precisely because of its messianic function. It did not both-
er him that the leading Zionists and most of the early
immigrants were not religious. He regarded them as
tools for a good cause, which in the end would come to
view the actual task of Zionism as a religious-messianic
movement and change course. Kook himself remained a
well respected, albeit solitary thinker, but the far more
radical ideas of his son, Rabbi Zvi Yehuda Kook (1891–

1982), would build the ideological foundation for the settlement movement in the occupied territories after the Six Day War in 1967. Only since that time has the national-religious movement been considered the precursor of a messianic national position within Zionism. The early religious Zionists had tried to gain a place at least at the margins of organized Zionism by putting aside the messianic element, but one hundred years later religious Zionists regarded themselves as the actual avant-garde of the movement precisely because of their messianic role.

Economic Order

One final factor that distinguished the various parties from one another was the issue of economic order in the future Jewish state. In this matter, the primary adversaries were the socialist Zionists and their middle-class counterparts from the Revisionist camp. Socialist Zionism, which was modelled on the social revolutionary ideology in Russia, stood for the most diverse forms of collective co-existence intended to create a new social order in Palestine. In the *kvuzot*, or, as they were later called, *kibbutzim*, not only would private possessions be taboo, but the traditional nuclear family would be diffused with special children's houses, and mental effort would be coupled with physical labor. This ideology impelled the pioneer spirit of the first settlers, but the

vast majority of the immigrants resided outside of socialist model settlements of this sort.

The Histadrut, a federation of Jewish workers founded in 1920, had a far more sweeping significance. In the
1930s and 1940s, about three quarters of all organized
workers in Palestine belonged to it. The term "worker"
was expanded to comprise teachers, office workers, and
freelancers, who also qualified for membership in this
union. David Ben-Gurion was probably correct in char-
acterizing the Histadrut not as a union, but as an alliance of the builders of the homeland, founders of the
state, revitalizers of the nation, and creators of the future. The Histadrut was more than a federation of workers. Its extraordinary significance distinguished it from
any similar institution in a democratic state.

The Revisionists directed their disdain not only at the
worker's party itself, but also at the institutions associated with it, such as the labor union. Jabotinsky and his
supporters advocated a middle-class society that did not
involve labor union predominance. In doing so, they
chalked up successes among the Polish Jews, both those
who had emigrated to Palestine and the Zionists who
remained active in Poland during the interwar years.

Nevertheless, the position of the socialist camp by the
beginning of the early 1930s came increasingly to set
the tone. In the early 1920s, the General Zionists, who
were elected by means of national lists, still constituted
a clear majority of the delegates at the Congresses, but
in 1933 the socialist camp had by far the greatest per-

centage, with 44 percent of all elected delegates. In Palestine, they even attained 71 percent of all votes at that time. Jabotinsky's Revisionists dropped back that same year from 25 percent of the votes to 14 percent. Until the time of the Israeli parliamentary elections in 1977, the left camp did not relinquish its dominance in Zionist or, later, Israeli politics.

CHAPTER FIVE

The Long Path to the Jewish State: Palestine as British Mandate

A poster calling for the establishment of a Jewish army during the period of the British Mandate in Palestine.

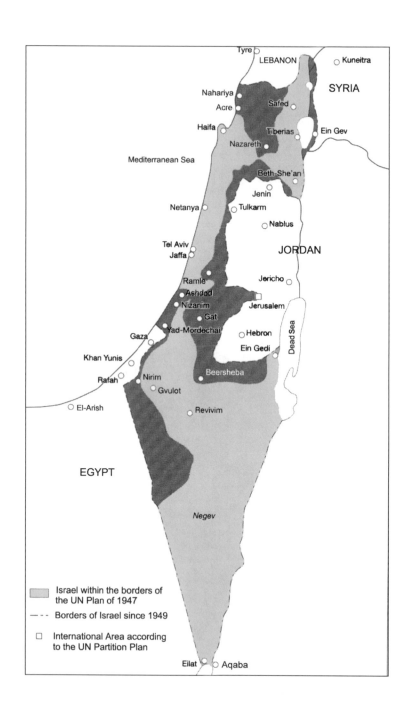

Tyre

LEBANON

Kuneitra

SYRIA

Nahariya

Safed

Acre

Haifa

Tiberias

Ein Gev

Nazareth

Mediterranean Sea

Beth-She'an

Jenin

Netanya

Tulkarm

Nablus

Tel Aviv

JORDAN

Jaffa

Ramle

Jericho

Ashdod

Nizanim

Jerusalem

Gat

Yad-Mordechai

Gaza

Hebron

Khan Yunis

Ein Gedi

Rafah

Nirim

Beersheba

Gvulot

Dead Sea

El-Arish

Revivim

EGYPT

Negev

Israel within the borders of
the UN Plan of 1947

Borders of Israel since 1949

International Area according
to the UN Partition Plan

Eilat

Aqaba

After the First World War, a crucial transformation in the circumstances of the Jewish minority began to unfold in East Central Europe. Before the war, the overwhelming majority of the European Jews had lived in three multinational empires: Tsarist Russia, the Habsburg Dual Monarchy, and the Ottoman Empire. They had constituted one among many minorities and could preserve elements of their national autonomy with their own language (Yiddish or Ladino), their own educational system, and some features of their own jurisdiction. When these empires disintegrated, the European Jews were confronted with a new set of circumstances. Salonika, which had a large Jewish community with a rich cultural tradition, became part of Greece, where the position of Jews was worse than in Ottoman society, on the eve of the First World War. This development foreshadowed similar phenomena on a larger scale after the war in new states such as Yugoslavia and Czechoslovakia, in the Baltic states, and in reestablished Poland. Their claim to national sovereignty, which was a central demand in the Paris peace negotiations in 1919, was quite difficult to implement in practice. It soon became clear that either artificial states like Yugoslavia would need to be created or, as in Poland, over one third of the population would have to be integrated as national minorities (Jews, Germans, Ukrainians). They were no longer subject to the Tsar, Emperor, or Sultan, but at the mercy of the dominant majority, which defined the nation. In practice, this often entailed cultural and economic subordination for the minorities and even exclusion and persecution.

In the Soviet Union, on the other hand, after a brief initial blossoming of Jewish culture, the atheistic state persecuted all organized religions, particularly when it came to smaller minorities. Political instability that resulted from the rise of fascism and National Socialism in Central Europe targeted the Jews specifically or as one group among others. Antisemitic incidents in Germany and Austria also had a more marked impact on everyday Jewish life than in the prewar years. In light of these developments it is hardly surprising that Zionism gained supporters throughout Europe in the interwar years. For one thing, political recognition by the Balfour Declaration lent an undreamt-of respectability to this movement, which had often been derided in the past as utopian, and for another, younger Jews in particular grew uncertain about their bonds with their respective homelands as they were increasingly excluded from non-Jewish society.

Zionism in the Diaspora

German-speakers were the leaders of the Zionist organization from its beginnings to the end of World War I. Although they constituted only a small minority of the movement, and Zionists were a minority among German-speaking Jews, Zionists from Germany were represented disproportionately in leadership roles. During those years, perhaps fewer than ten percent of all German Jews considered themselves part of the Zionist movement, and a significant portion of those Jews came from Eastern Europe. The first generation of German Zionists defined its primary task as the support of emigration of Eastern European Jews. It was not until a younger generation had gained influence in the Zionistische Vereinigung für Deutschland in the years preceding World War I under the leadership of Kurt Blumenfeld that this Zionist movement made the principle of planning for its own future in Palestine part of its platform. The actual number of German Zionists who emigrated to Palestine before 1933 was extremely small, around 3,000 between 1920 and 1932.

Even though the number of active Zionists in Germany in the 1920s did not rise markedly and stayed within a range that did not exceed 20,000, Zionism did gain supporters, particularly in the context of so-called *Gegenwartsarbeit*. This German term denoted "Zionist work in the present," the reinforcement of Jewish national ideology among Jews who were remaining in the Diaspora for the time being, but would participate in building a new Jewish society. Central to *Gegenwartsarbeit* in the Diaspora was Theodor Herzl's call for the "conquest of communities." Before the First World War, the Jewish communities in Germany were essentially either Reform or Orthodox, and both rejected Zionism as a political movement. When the right to vote was democratized in the Weimar Republic, a shift of emphasis favored the Jüdische Volkspartei, which was controlled by Zionists. In their local elections they were at times able to chalk up astonishing successes. In Berlin in the late 1920s, an active Zionist, Georg Kareski, was appointed board president of the largest Jewish community in Germany. In Vienna there was an even more striking development that favored the Zionist parties, which constituted the majority in the religious community after 1932. In Germany and Austria, the success of Zionism was measured less in the number of emigrants than in the transformation of the self-image of the Jewish population, the successful development of the Jewish educational system, and the recasting of some Jewish religious communities as *Volksgemeinden* (ethnic communities), which addressed far more than just the religious needs of its members.

An additional boon to Zionism in Central Europe was the inclusion of non-Zionists in Zionist committees, particularly those concerned with the issue of building Palestine. The Palestine Foundation Fund (Keren Hayesod), established in 1920 for this purpose, pursued an unusual course of action in its German branch, founded two years later, by going to great lengths to include non-Zionist dignitaries, in particular Rabbi Leo Baeck, the banker Oskar Wassermann, and representatives of large Jewish organizations and communities. The Zionists had to relinquish some control over building Palestine, but by doing so they expanded the basis of their activities and made Zionism socially acceptable in an environment that might best be described as wary.

Zionism in Eastern Europe during the interwar period had little in common with the situation in Germany. In the Soviet Union, after an initial brief acceptance of the Hebrew language and Jewish cultural endeavors, all Zionist activities were banned by the Jewish section of the Communist Party (the *Yevsektsia*). The history of Zionism would certainly have turned out differently if Zionist activity had been possible in this center of prewar Zionism, which had nearly three million Jewish citizens. In most of East Central Europe, on the other hand, the breeding ground for the Zionist movement was close to ideal. The exceptions were areas with a strictly orthodox population, such as the extreme east of Czechoslovakia and the Maramures region of Romania, as well as places with a highly assimilated Jewish population, such as parts of Bohemia and Hungary. In general, however, East Central Europe between the world wars was the center not only of Zionist activities, but also of emigration to Palestine. The Zionist movement was also bolstered by the fact that small ethnic groups such as the Estonians and Latvians achieved statehood after the First World War, and the old nation of Poland was restored. In this situation, many people concluded that the hour of the Zionists had arrived. Besides conquering the community centers, the Zionists set out to disseminate the Hebrew language throughout the Diaspora and to mobilize young people for emigration.

In Czechoslovakia, Zionism achieved special prominence owing to President Tomas Masaryk's benevolent attitude toward this movement. Three Zionist Congresses took place here during the interwar period, two in Carlsbad and one in Prague. The writer Max Brod was active in the Zionist-oriented Jewish Council of Czechoslovakia, which was formed in Prague in 1918. Later the Jewish Party, led by Zionists, won a seat in the Prague parliament. In Hungary, the reform-minded Neologs (Hungarian Modern Reform Movement) contested the Zionist Association, which did not attain legal status until 1927. The number of emigrants was limited in both countries, as well as in neighboring Romania, in which Zionist representatives were also elected into the Parliament. Lithuania had the highest percentage of active Zionists as well as emigrants to Palestine. In this small country, only a minute percentage of the Jewish population identified with the dominant language and culture, and there were very few Jewish opponents of Zionism, mainly orthodox Jews.

The approximately three million Polish Jews constituted the center of Zionist activities. Most regarded themselves as a distinct ethnic group. They spoke their own language and felt a traditional kinship with the land of Israel, which provided a very different basis for Zionist activity from German Jews who defined themselves as German citizens of the Jewish faith. The Polish Parliament, the Sejm, sometimes had over 30 Zionist delegates. The numerous Jewish media were mostly pro-

Zionist. The Zionist youth movement numbered over 100,000 members, and more than 40,000 children were being educated in the Hebrew-language Tarbut schools. The total number of emigrants to Palestine in the inter-war period, about 140,000, was, however, a small fraction of the Polish Jewish population between 1919 and 1942. At the same time, the political differences in Poland within the Jewish communities and within Zionism itself were more pronounced than in Western Europe. Assimilationists, Orthodox Jews, Bundists, and autonomists competed with the deeply divided Zionist groups. Of these, Vladimir Jabotinsky's middle-class Revisionists attracted large numbers of Jewish members in the 1920s. Only in South Africa did the Revisionists have a comparable impact. There, Zionist engagement was especially prominent despite the relatively small Jewish population. During the 1920s, South African per capita donations for the Keren Hayesod were the highest in the world. By 1930, 200 organizations were allied with the association of South African Zionists.

In the Jewish communities of Northern Africa and the Middle East, a messianic yearning to return to the Holy Land had traditionally remained strong. However, here too, political Zionism was soon able to gain a foothold, often under the influence of European emissaries. Delegates from Algeria, Tunisia, and Egypt began participating as early as the Second Zionist Congress in 1898. Between World War I and World War II, the Zionist youth organizations became particularly active. The success of the actual emigration depended in no small part on the living conditions in the various countries. In the three decades preceding the founding of the State of Israel, about 14,000 Jews immigrated to Palestine from Yemen, about 10,000 from Syria, and 8,000 from Iraq. By contrast, only a few hundred immigrated from Algeria. The political heightening of the Palestinian conflict and eventually the foundation of the State of Israel led to rioting against the local Jewish population, which at times turned quite fierce.

During the interwar period, the Zionist Organization of America grew to be the largest Zionist group. In contrast to Eastern European Jews, very few Jews in America were actually interested in emigrating to Palestine. Most of them had immigrated quite recently and did not wish to consider a second emigration. Of course there were exceptions, such as the future Israeli Prime Minister Golda Myerson (Meir), who was born in Kiev and grew up in Milwaukee before settling on a kibbutz in Palestine in 1921. As a rule, however, the American Zionists were distinguished by their philanthropic engagement rather than an activist stance. Founded in defiance of the explicit resistance of the German-American Jewish establishment, Zionist organizations in the United States initially fought for social acceptance. It was therefore crucial that in addition to the eminent men who were active in the Zionist New York Achavah Club, Zionist circles were developing at major universities in Boston, namely Harvard, Tufts, and Boston University.

Against the background of the burning of books in Germany and the Arab Revolt in Palestine, this poster from New York (1937) calls American Jews to make their "Shekel" contributions to the Zionist cause.

The breakthrough of American Zionism as a force to be reckoned with came when the prominent attorney Louis D. Brandeis was elected head of the Federation of American Zionists in 1914. His appointment to the Supreme Court of the United States two years later spelled the end of his official Zionist activities, but at the same time signified a tremendous victory for the cause of Zionism.

Inspired in no small part by his encounter with the Irish population in Boston, which fought for the independence of its fellow countrymen, Brandeis identified with Zionism as a Jew rooted in America, without ever contemplating emigration himself. In a 1915 speech he formulated his reasons for Zionist engagement, which applied equally to many other American Zionists: "Multiple loyalties are objectionable only if they are inconsistent. A man is a better citizen of the United States for being also a loyal citizen of his state, and of his city; for being loyal to his family, and to his profession or trade; for being loyal to his college or lodge. . . . Every American Jew who aids in advancing the Jewish settlement in Palestine, though he feels that neither he nor his descendants will ever live there, will be a better man and a better American for doing so."[61] Notable in the development of American Zionism was the unique engagement of the women's organization Hadassah. Under the leadership of Henrietta Szold, Hadassah, which had about 40,000 members in 1927, was devoted primarily to setting up health services in Palestine.

The Zionist movement, the headquarters of which had been temporarily relocated to neutral Copenhagen during the war years, gained both a new central office in London and a new President, Chaim Weizmann, when the war ended. At a conference held in London in 1920, there were confrontations between the contrasting personalities of Weizmann and Brandeis. Weizmann bluntly declared to Brandeis: "I do not agree with the philosophy of your Zionism. . . . We are different, absolutely different. There is no bridge between Washington and Pinsk."[62]

This was a clash not only of political ideas, but of styles. The pragmatic Brandeis had trouble enduring the long and often tiresome Congress addresses, and made no attempt to hide his distaste. Brandeis believed that the major political demand of Zionism had been met with the Balfour Declaration, and that it was now feasible to focus on building up Palestine. His vision of an administration that was as decentralized as possible and ought to become active from Jerusalem and not from London diverged markedly from those of Weizmann and other European Zionists.

Brandeis could not prevail against Weizmann in the international Zionist organization with his plans for an economic construction of Palestine, and in 1921 his followers also lost the leadership of the Federation of American Zionists. The American Zionists, who constituted the most important financial resource in the Zionist movement, were derailed by incessant infighting in the 1920s and 1930s. Not until the forceful leadership of Reform Rabbis Stephen Wise and Abba Hillel Silver were they able to assume an active role within Zionism at a time in which the Jews of Europe were already in an acute state of crisis.

The more significant power struggle within Zionism during the interwar years would not be waged between London and New York, however, but between London and Jerusalem. Weizmann remained the top representative of the Zionist movement until the founding of the State of Israel, despite the challenge of his various internal opponents such as Brandeis and Jabotinsky and notwithstanding the fact that Nahum Sokolow replaced him as the nominal head of the international organization from 1931 to 1935. However, he was becoming an "elder statesman" who was gradually losing his control over everyday political affairs, because Zionist policy for Palestine was being guided more and more from Jerusalem itself, and David Ben-Gurion held the reins there. The constellation of 1948, when Weizmann took on a largely symbolic role with the office of President, while Ben-Gurion's office of Prime Minister had all the political power, had been evolving during the two preceding decades.

Palestine under the British

During the First World War, nearly 20,000 Jews left Palestine, some of their own accord, but more often under duress. They were citizens of a great many countries, and had to don the uniforms of the European armies. Many former neighbors from Jaffa or an agricultural collective in Galilee now encountered one another on European battlegrounds across enemy lines. Palestine itself was on the periphery of the major events of the war, although here too deplorable conditions prevailed toward the end of the war and a famine began to exact many victims, especially in the Arab population. The Allies took precautions even before the conquest of the Middle East to divide the territories to be taken over from the "sick man of Europe" (the Ottoman Empire). According to the Sykes-Picot Agreement of May 9, 1916, France would control southern Anatolia up to Mosul, Acre, and Damascus, and the British would receive the territory just south of this area from Amman to Baghdad. An international zone was proposed for the Christian holy places in Palestine and surrounding territory. At the same time, the British made promises to both Jews and Arabs. In addition to the Balfour Declaration, the High Commissioner in Egypt, Henry McMahon, promised Sharif Husayn of Mecca an Arab kingdom comprising almost all of Arab western Asia. However, McMahon's letter was just as vaguely worded as Balfour's declaration regarding a Jewish homeland in

Palestine. It failed to mention whether Palestine is included in this Arab state.

The diplomatic success of Zionism continued during
the years immediately following the war. The San Remo
Conference in 1920 decided to assign the mandate for
Palestine under the League of Nations to Great Britain
on the basis of the Balfour Declaration, officially recognizing the Zionist Organization as the Jewish Agency
and requiring the mandatory power to facilitate Jewish
immigration. In so doing, the pledge given by the British Foreign Secretary to create a national home for the
Jews became an international legal agreement. In the
decades to follow, the Zionists would be fighting to ensure that this pledge was honored—and learning
the hard way that Balfour's formulation was highly in-
determinate.

The early stages boded well. After a transitional phase
between 1917 and 1920, in which Palestine was gov-
erned by a British military administration, Great Britain
sent a Jewish former cabinet minister, Sir Herbert Samuel, to Jerusalem as the first High Commissioner. Many
Zionists interpreted the fact that a Jew, who moreover
was favorably disposed to Zionism, was holding the
highest political office in Palestine as a positive sign and
even as the dawn of a new era. The fact that the mandate provided for the recognition of a Jewish Agency as
a public corporate body to cooperate with the administration on economic, political, and other matters was
also regarded as a promising new beginning. Soon, how-

ever, less encouraging tendencies in British policy emerged. Winston Churchill, who was the British Colonial Secretary at the time, made clear in a 1922 White Paper that England did not intend to have Palestine become "as Jewish as England is English."[63] The immigration of Jews would be permitted as long as it did not exceed the economic capacity of the country. Moreover, the White Paper attempted to clarify the Balfour Declaration, but still remained fairly vague: "When it is asked what is meant by the development of the Jewish National Home in Palestine, it may be answered that it is not the imposition of a Jewish nationality upon the inhabitants of Palestine as a whole, but the further development of the existing Jewish community, with the assistance of Jews in other parts of the world, in order that it may become a centre in which the Jewish people as a whole may take, on grounds of religion and race, an interest and pride."[64]

Transjordan (now called Jordan) was separated from the mandate as a result of the White Paper. Although the Zionists did not greet this decision with enthusiasm, they accepted it. What made them much more upset with Sir Samuel was his reaction to the Arab unrest of 1921 by calling a temporary halt to immigration.

A sense of crisis also loomed within Zionism in the early 1920s. Only one-third of the one and a half million pounds that were envisaged at the 1923 Zionist Conference was collected, the number of immigrants to Palestine (fewer than 10,000 per year) lay far below expectations, and Russian Zionists such as Ussishkin and Jabotinsky accused Weizmann of remaining too docile toward the British. People were beginning to realize that even now that diplomatic recognition had been achieved, affluent Jews were not donating generous sums of money, Eastern Europeans were not emigrating to Palestine in large numbers, and any apparent unity of the Zionist movement was only an illusion.

Nevertheless, Zionism was able to achieve a degree of success even in those years. Weizmann's big moment came on August 11, 1929, when he convened the inaugural meeting of an expanded Jewish Agency, as provided for in the mandate for Palestine. Its Jerusalem Executive would be in charge of immigration to Palestine, land purchase, and cultural development. After years of negotiations, Weizmann succeeded in bringing prominent non-Zionists into the Agency. They included Albert Einstein, the future French Premier Léon Blum, and the long-standing President of the American Jewish Committee, Louis Marshall. In the long term, however, they were unable to render the Agency independent from the World Zionist Organization, as they had hoped. The Jewish Agency essentially became the executive branch of the World Zionist Organization, and the two organizations shared a board of directors.

Their joy in founding the "Jewish Agency" faded after only a few weeks of its existence. Louis Marshall, one of its mainstays, died soon after, the stock market crash on Wall Street had negative repercussions for building

Palestine, and in Palestine itself the worst riots since the beginning of the mandatory era broke out in August 1929. These riots were triggered by conflicts concerning the status of the Western Wall. In the preceding years, Muslims had complained that setting out chairs for the elderly and erecting a dividing screen for women and men violated the status quo. When Arab construction work around the Western Wall aroused the indignation of the Jewish population, several hundred young Jewish demonstrators of the Betar movement organized protest marches. On August 23, Arabs attacked Jews after Friday prayers; riots began to spread to other cities, and within a week, a total of 133 Jews, of whom 60 were from Hebron alone, were murdered, and several hundred injured. On the Arab side, 116 deaths and about 100 injuries were recorded.

The events of August 1929 marked a turning point in the relations between Jews and Arabs in Palestine. Although there had been repeated isolated clashes, the outbreaks of violence sanctioned by the mufti of Jerusalem would form the initial link in a chain of events that overshadowed all political initiatives in Palestine during the 1930s. Even the British government, represented by a new High Commissioner, Sir John Chancellor, was unable to nip this conflict in the bud. New commissions continued to be sent from London to Palestine during the 1930s to work out solutions, generally in the form of plans for partition, but they all came to naught.

Immediately following the riots of August 1929, the

British Colonial Secretary Lord Passfield appointed an investigatory commission. Its March 1930 report—the Shaw Report—emphasized Arab responsibility for the massacres, but also singled out Jewish immigration, which, it said, exceeded the absorptive capacity of the country, as a crucial factor in creating instability. The British government wobbled on the Passfield White Paper of 1930, which signified a departure from the Balfour Declaration. This was reversed in the MacDonald Letter of 1931. But the episode had repercussions within the Zionist movement as well. Weizmann increasingly came under fire as pro-British. When he distanced himself from the call for a Jewish majority in Palestine in an interview during the Zionist Congress of 1931, the majority of the delegates reacted by agreeing to a vote of no confidence against Weizmann. However, since his opponents were deeply divided and his followers continued to constitute the largest faction, the result was a new team favorably inclined toward Weizmann with Nahum Sokolow at its head. Weizmann himself was once again elected the head of the Zionist Organization four years later.

An unprecedented rate of immigration to Palestine occurred during this turbulent period. The reason was not the improved living conditions in the new homeland, but the immediate danger in the old one. The National Socialist takeover in Germany and the threat to neighboring countries brought 37,000 new immigrants to the land in 1933, 45,000 in 1934, and 66,000 in 1935. In only three years, the Jewish population of Palestine virtually doubled, and an expansion particularly of the three cities of Tel Aviv, Jerusalem, and Haifa made rapid progress during this period. In contrast to the Jews from Eastern Europe, the German immigrants had not opted to come to Palestine for reasons of Zionist idealism, but in response to a tangible threat. This was expressed in a popular joke among the Jewish population of Palestine: "Are you coming out of conviction or out of Germany?" Because of British restrictions, however, the number of immigrants fell rapidly beginning in the mid-1930s, in which a safe refuge would have been especially important. In 1936 there were fewer than 30,000 immigrants, in 1937 about 10,000, and only a few more in the two years that followed. The immigrants from German-speaking countries constituted only about 2.5 percent of the immigration until 1933, but their share rose to over 70 percent per year by the end of the 1930s.

The high numbers of immigrants until the mid-1930s were the primary impetus for a major Arab revolt in 1936, which began as a general strike and developed into riots against Jews and eventually a full-scale rebellion against British rule. According to the leader of the Palestine Arab nationalist movement, the mufti of Jerusalem, Haj Amin al-Husayni, the whole Zionist experiment ought to be declared a failure and broken off. He argued for a complete end to immigration, an end to the mandate and the Jewish National Home, and the proclamation of an Arab state in Palestine.

However, larger political developments in the region as a whole also contributed to the unrest in 1936. Arab nationalism had gotten a fresh impetus from the foundation of new Arab states. The British had granted Transjordan and Egypt partial sovereignty. France had also made concessions to the states under its dominion. After Feisal, the son of the sharif of Mecca, had been deposed following a brief intermezzo as King of Syria, the French combined the two small states of Aleppo and Damascus into Syria in 1925, and Lebanon was granted greater autonomy in 1926. In 1932, Iraq (where Feisal was named king by the British, who made his brother Abdullah the emir of Transjordan) was granted formal independence. These developments, which were more in the nature of symbolic politics than of power politics, raised both Jewish and Arab political expectations of the mandatory power. The Zionists anticipated that the British would now make good on the Balfour Declaration and allow for a Jewish state in Palestine analogous to the Arab states in the region. On the other side, an Arab-Palestinian state also appeared to be within reach.

As the political situation in Europe worsened, the Axis powers Germany and Italy attempted to capitalize on the complicated situation of the British. Mussolini intensified his claims to greater influence in the eastern Mediterranean region from his African bases in Libya and Ethiopia, while Hitler tried to further the German position in the Arab world by means of cultural and economic activities. In addition to emphasizing the foe they had in common, the National Socialists attempted to bolster pan-Arabic endeavors, especially by bringing them into line with the creation of a greater German empire.

The British thus found themselves in a political predicament. On the one hand, they had come out in favor of the establishment of a Jewish home in Palestine in the Balfour Declaration of 1917 and they recognized the growing necessity for this kind of step in view of the government-sanctioned antisemitism that was rapidly spreading in Europe. On the other hand, they feared loss of influence in the Arab world at a time that conflict with the fascist powers was approaching. The British were keenly aware that the Jews would have no alternative but to fight on the side of the British and against the Germans in the event of a world war, while the Arab world was not an automatic ally. This consideration would dominate British Middle East policy during the 1930s and the wartime period. This meant revoking the promises made in the Balfour Declaration and attempting to keep the Palestine conflict under control by drastically restricting the numbers of Jewish immigrants.

Partition Plans

The violence that began in April 1936 lasted three years and had a more profound impact than the earlier ones in 1921 and 1929. Once individual disturbances on both sides had begun to escalate, an Arab Higher Committee, set up by the Grand Mufti of Jerusalem, decided to cease tax payments and to call a general strike. Not until the British government promised to send over an investigatory commission that would listen to the Arab complaints did the mufti call off the strike on October 11, 1936. Under the chairmanship of a former British Secretary of State for India, Earl Peel, the six commission members arrived in Palestine in November 1936. After five months of careful work, questioning Jewish, Arab, and British witnesses and inspecting documents, the commission published its report, which was over 400 pages long, in July 1937. The result amounted to an admission that the British promises to the Arabs and Jews could not be fulfilled within the framework of a single state. Only a drastic change in the existing situation could be at least somewhat fair. Professor Reginald Coupland, who was probably the most influential member of the commission, depicted the extent of the change by emphasizing: "There needs to be an operation; no honest doctor will recommend aspirins and a hot-water bottle."[65] Weizmann understood too well what this operation entailed for the patient: being split in two. A Solomonic judgment, however, was out of the question in this situation.

The Peel Commission's first recommendation was to divide Palestine into an Arab and a Jewish state with mandatory enclaves (particularly Jerusalem and a strip of land to the coast south of Jaffa and the area around Nazareth). While being far from an ideal solution, this was the decisive breakthrough towards the acceptance of the idea of a Jewish state. For the rest of the century, in different variants, partition remained on the political agenda as a solution for Palestine.

After expressing initial reserve regarding the planned mini-state, which would comprise a narrow coastal strip between Tel Aviv and the border to Lebanon as well as Galilee, the Zionist Congress of 1937 recommended (over the bitter protests of Jabotinsky, Ussishkin, and an influential minority group) pursuing this opportunity for independent statehood. Weizmann considered it the only realistic chance of securing a state in the foreseeable future, and Ben-Gurion saw it as a starting point for a state that would later expand. The Arabs, however, made no secret of their fundamental rejection of this solution. They demanded an immediate halt to immigration and the founding of a Palestinian state as long as there was still an Arab majority.

In the meantime, the British also dissociated themselves from the recommendations of the Peel Commission. One of its sharpest critics was Viscount Herbert Samuel, who in the House of Lords pointed out many shortcomings and argued for the creation of a large confederation of Arab states of which the Jewish national home might form a part without provoking Arab nationalism. In September 1937 Lewis Andrews, the District Commissioner of Galilee and Acre, was shot to death in Nazareth by Arab nationalists. This set off a new wave of violence as well as repression from the British. The British sent over a new commission, led by Sir John Woodhead, to prepare a detailed plan for partition. However, this commission was boycotted by the Arab nationalists. On November 9, 1938, the British Parliament received the commission's report, which rejected the Peel Plan as unrealistic. The Woodhead Report nevertheless proposed various alternative partition schemes, providing for a smaller Jewish state. Just two days later, however, the British Cabinet rejected any partition of Palestine and arrived at the banal conclusion that "the surest foundation for peace and progress in Palestine would be an understanding between the Arabs and the Jews."[66] This trite finding surely did not merit several commissions and hundreds of pages of official reports.

As these decisions were being reached, synagogues were burning in Germany, and tens of thousands of German Jews were being sent to concentration camps. It was still possible for them to regain their freedom, assuming that they had an entry permit for a foreign country. In this situation, however, access to Palestine was being cut off. The largest and most momentous setback to date, not only for the Zionists, but for European

Jews as a whole, was the Round Table Conference in London's St. James's Palace, convened in February 1939. There were essentially two conferences, since the Arab representatives refused to sit at the same table as the Jews. The failure of these discussions led to the publication in May 1939 of a new White Paper, which was to determine British policies in Palestine for the war years. The introduction explained that the Balfour Declaration had never intended the founding of a Jewish state against the will of the Arab populace. It went on to state that the British government would enable Palestine to gain independence within ten years. In order to ensure that an Arab majority would continue, a quota was set of 10,000 Jewish immigrants for each of the next five years plus a total of 25,000 additional Jewish refugees. After this period, no further Jewish immigrants would be allowed into the country without Arab consent. Moreover, severe restrictions would be placed on the sale of land to Jews.

This outcome was a devastating blow for Weizmann personally and for Zionism as a whole. It also demonstrated the powerlessness of world Jewry vis-à-vis the British government and marked an end to the hopes of millions of European Jews who were threatened by National Socialism. In a bitterly ironic twist, the end of Jewish emigration was set for the year 1944, when the gas chambers of Auschwitz were running at full capacity and virtually nothing was left of the major Jewish communities from Vilnius and Salonika to Warsaw and

Amsterdam. David Ben-Gurion portrayed the new situation as follows: "For centuries, Jews were asking themselves in their prayers: 'When will there be a state for our people once again?' But nobody would ever have thought of posing the awful question: 'Will our people still exist when this state comes to being?'"

The policies of Ben-Gurion and the Zionist leadership in regard to rescue operations for the European Jews threatened by annihilation have been subject to increased critical analysis in recent years. Critiques of this sort typically point out that Ben-Gurion's priority of establishing a Jewish state ran at cross-purposes with possible rescue operations outside of the Zionist framework. Even these critics, however, essentially accept the fact that the stateless Zionist leadership during World War II had limited means of exerting political pressure at its disposal.

Whether they wished to or not, the Zionists had to wage war side by side with the British mandatory power against antisemitic Germany. The British, on the other hand, could actively seek allies in the Arab states, since the latter had often made it quite clear that they could pursue other options. The Grand Mufti of Jerusalem was received by Hitler on November 30, 1941 and repeatedly used German radio stations to appeal to the Arabs to support the National Socialists. When Rommel advanced into Egypt, the Jewish population of Palestine prepared for the worst. The Carmel Plan, devised at this time, contemplated armed Jewish defense within a strip of land in northern Palestine after a British withdrawal.

Shortly before Rommel's army was defeated at al-Alamein, thus averting the danger for the Jews of Palestine, about 600 Zionist delegates, most of whom were Americans, gathered in May 1942 for an emergency conference at the Biltmore Hotel in New York. The Biltmore Program, supported by Ben-Gurion, sounded a more aggressive tone than previous Zionist announcements. Referring to the Balfour Declaration and expressing an explicit wish to cooperate with the Arab nations, it rejected the British White Paper of 1939, and reaffirmed the right of the Jews to their own state. At the same time, however, it was also testimony to their helplessness in the face of the most trying times in Jewish history. As long as the war against Germany went on, the hands of the Zionists, with the exception of some extremists, were tied when it came to the British. When the war ended, however, the British were no longer regarded as allies, but occupiers, against whom an underground battle would now be waged.

At first Zionist resistance consisted of organizing illegal immigration of Jewish refugees into Palestine, which continued to be blocked by the British. In early 1946, the number of "illegals" exceeded one thousand per month. After that, however, the British intensified their naval blockade and detained a total of 26,000 Jewish refugees in internment camps on Cyprus. The return of the refugee ship *Exodus 1947* filled with 4,500 Jewish Displaced Persons to Germany of all places was the most shocking development. The fact that Holocaust survivors after their liberation from concentration camps were now being held against their will in German and Cypriot internment camps and were prevented from immigrating to Palestine undoubtedly had an inestimable moral significance in the political decision to establish a Jewish state.

In addition to abetting illegal immigration, the Zionists offered active resistance to British policies concerning Palestine. The ensuing violence culminated in the summer of 1946. After the British had begun systematically to combat Zionist underground activities on the so-called Black Sabbath (June 29, 1946), the right-wing Irgun Zvai Leumi (National Military Organization), an underground troup inspired by Revisionist Zionism and led by Menachem Begin, responded on July 22, 1946 by bombing the King David Hotel in Jerusalem, which was occupied by the British administration. There were 91 casualties, British, Jewish, and Arab. Two years after the war ended, the British realized that they could no longer fulfil their mandate in Palestine, even with a reinforced military presence, in the face of bitter Jewish and Arab resistance. Questions concerning the future of Palestine were referred to the United Nations, in the hands of which lay the destiny of both peoples.

Zionism or Post-Zionism? The Zionist Idea after the Founding of the State of Israel

A New Year's greeting card printed in Paris in 1949 depicts a luxury liner full of immigrants arriving in the Land of Israel, bearing the name of the most renowned immigrant vessel, the Exodus.

At the beginning of the third millennium and one century after Theodor Herzl's initial political endeavors to found a Jewish state, Israel can look back on a history that is regarded as a success story for some, and for others as an experiment threatened by failure. The optimists point out that Israel has developed an island of western democracy amidst an autocratically ruled region. At the beginning of the 21st century, Israel is economically superior to many a European region and is one of the culturally most diverse societies with immigrants from over a hundred different countries. The pessimists, by contrast, see a state that is plagued by numerous wars and threats from without. It is a state in which the military has a high profile, a state torn apart by internal conflicts between the religious and the secular, Europeans and Orientals, Arabs and Jews, political extremists and moderates.

Both optimists and pessimists can lay claim to a grain of truth. Particularly for the generation of Holocaust survivors, it borders on the miraculous that in such a brief period of time after the darkest chapter of Jewish history, a Jewish state has been brought to life once again for the first time after almost 2,000 years. This state has endured for five decades in an environment that has not been kindly disposed to it. The mass immigration of almost a million people from the former Soviet Union during the 1990s would seem to confirm that the dream of returning to Zion lives on. However, the statistics also show that the immigrants came to

Israel primarily from economically and politically un-
stable systems, while only a minute percentage immigrated from the largest Jewish community in the world,
the United States. In fact, more Israelis have emigrated
to North America in the past few decades than the other
way around.

A State Without Peace

On November 29, 1947, it appeared that the Zionist
ideal had been achieved. Hundreds of thousands of Jews
who had immigrated to Palestine were glued to their
radios to await the decision of the United Nations General Assembly on the partition of Palestine. Only a short
time earlier it had been uncertain as to whether there
would be the majority necessary for the UN to decide on
a resolution that would partition Palestine into a Jewish
and an Arab state with an international zone around
Jerusalem. As had been the case in the British partition
plans of the 1930s, the Zionist leadership had struggled
to arrive at territorial compromises that were light years
removed from their true aspirations, but finally brought
a Jewish state within reach. The Arab states and their
allies, on the other hand, expressed their frank opposition to a partition of Palestine and the foundation of a
Jewish state that would result from it. They regarded a
Jewish state as a foreign element in the Middle East. The
position of the great powers was unclear up to the last

minute. While Great Britain abstained in its capacity as mandatory power, the Soviet Union voted for partition, most likely in order to remove British influence from the area. The United States, later to become Israel's closest ally, hesitated right up to the last minute. Its vote and those of numerous smaller states ultimately ensured passage of the United Nations resolution, which was slated to take effect half a year later, in May 1948.

The implementation of the UN partition resolution applied only to the State of Israel. The Arab Palestinian state, which was also planned, did not materialize because the armies of the Arab states attacked their new neighbor even before the State of Israel was founded. What became known as the West Bank was later annexed by Transjordan (renamed Jordan), while Egypt occupied the Gaza Strip. The War of Independence, which lasted almost a year, brought Israel territorial gains that included the western portion of Jerusalem, while the eastern part of the city, including the Old City and its religious sites, went to Jordan. Until the Old City was conquered by Israeli troops in the 1967 war, Jews were barred access to their holiest places. For the Palestinians, the war of 1948–49 resulted in a mass flight, the repercussions of which have marked the Palestinian tragedy to this day. Between 600,000 and 760,000 Palestinians lost their homes between December 1947 and September 1949. They fled not only to the Gaza Strip and the West Bank, but also to Jordan and Lebanon, where they have continued to live in refugee camps for decades. The Palestinian Diaspora in the Western world and in the Gulf States originated primarily in the nascent homelessness of those years.

The question whether their departure should be called flight or expulsion has been much debated. Recent historians find that it was a mixture of both factors. They counter both the traditional Israeli explanation, which framed the situation as a mass flight of the Palestinian populace urged upon them by their leaders, and the Arab interpretation, according to which the Israeli army organized the expulsion. These studies demonstrate that there was no systematic expulsion by the Israelis, though there were many cases of military expulsions at a local level. The fact that the Palestinians left the country was not unwelcome as far as the army was concerned, and the Palestinian departure was hastened by orders of the Haganah to expel Arabs from some villages. The Arab flight was further stimulated by the terrorist actions of the right-wing military groups, which were not supported by the official Israeli army. This terror reached its tragic height on April 9, 1948 in the massacre of the Arab civilian population in the village of Deir Yassin. There were over 200 casualties.

The myth of the triumph of David over a hapless Goliath was born in the War of Independence of 1948, and expanded in the Suez War of 1956 and in the Six-Day War of 1967. Although Israeli territorial gains from Egypt had to be given back in response to pressure from the superpowers (United States and the USSR), Israel did retain control of the formerly Jordanian West Bank, the formerly Egyptian Gaza Strip and Sinai Peninsula, and the formerly Syrian Golan Heights after June 1967. East Jerusalem and the Golan Heights were later annexed. The Sinai Peninsula was returned in stages to Egypt after the Camp David Accords in 1978, while the remaining territories remained under Israeli administration. However, Israel would now face its greatest long-term domestic political challenge when it came to control over the Palestinian Arab population living in these areas. The David who had fought to survive was now evolving into a Goliath in the eyes of the world, and this Goliath lost much moral credibility as an occupier. The selective settlement of the conquered territories, initially for military objectives, but later primarily for ideological and religious reasons, would, moreover, split apart Israeli society in regard to the ultimate status of those territories. Israel's most acerbic internal critic, the philosopher Yeshayahu Leibowitz, claimed: "Israel lost the Six-Day War on the seventh day."

The so-called Yom Kippur War of 1973 (named after the Jewish day of fasting on which the Egyptian and Syrian armies attacked) shattered the myth of Israel's invincibility, although the Israeli army eventually emerged from the Arab surprise attack superior to the Arab armies. However, Israeli vulnerability was showing, and this vulnerability became even more evident in the 1980s and 1990s. The Lebanon campaign of 1982 put Israeli society to a crucial test. For the first time, hundreds of thousands of Israelis took to the streets to protest the actions of their own army, which under Defense Minister Ariel Sharon did nothing to prevent Christian militiamen from massacring Palestinian refugees in the refugee camps of Sabra and Shatila. The Gulf War of 1991 and the sudden rocket attacks by Iraq made the renewed threat to the Israeli civilian population from without crystal clear. The idea that a whole people felt compelled to wear gas masks because they feared the use of chemical weapons also brought back memories of the darkest period of the Shoah. The intifada, a Palestinian rebellion against the Israeli occupiers between 1987 and 1993 that was carried out by youngsters throwing stones, showed that the traditional military superiority of Israel could barely cope with a popular uprising.

The hope that swelled after peace accords with Egypt (1979), Jordan (1994), and the Palestinians (1995) faded away with the assassination of Yitzhak Rabin (1995), the Prime Minister who focused on compromise, the subsequent wave of terror in Israel, the election of two right-wing governments (Netanyahu in 1996 and Sharon in 2001), and the outbreak of a second Palestinian uprising with increasing terror attacks in Israel's territory after the failure of the peace negotiations at Camp David (2000). Although for the first time several Arab states recognized Israel diplomatically and the Palestinians could rule with their own autonomous government in at least one part of their territory, the beginning of the

21st century did not bode well for a lasting peace to be achieved in the near future.

Pluralism or Discord?

Changes in foreign relations were followed by equally momentous upheavals within Israeli society. The Jewish residents of the State of Israel at the time of its founding were mostly of European descent, the majority of them from Eastern Europe. Even though this core population of the Jewish state was not homogeneous, either politically or socially, it was still united by common background, similar ideals, and in most cases the experience of the Shoah, to which the family members of many had fallen victim. In the 1950s, the massive immigration of Jews from Northern Africa and the Middle East began to alter the composition of the Israeli populace. Zionism as an ideological and political movement, as it has been depicted here, was an outgrowth of European nationalism. Although Zionism had also influenced segments of Jewry in Northern Africa and Asia Minor, the particular variety of Zionism in these areas was less modern and secular than traditional and religious. Moreover, during the first decades, many of the new immigrants were relegated to the background by the European establishment. Generally the dominance of the Ashkenazim was reflected in their economic and political pre-eminence and in their refusal to accept the

Northern African or Near Eastern culture of the non-
European Jews as equal.

Immigrants from Islamic countries expressed their
resentment by forming a non-political protest movement called the Black Panthers, which was modeled on
the American example. In the 1970s, their dissatisfac-
tion culminated in political upheaval within the parliamentary system. Until that time, the Labor Zionists had
retained uncontested governmental power, first under
founding father David Ben-Gurion, then under his successors Moshe Sharett, Levi Eshkol, Golda Meir, and
Yitzhak Rabin, though they always had to form coali-
tions with smaller partners. However, in 1977, the right-
wing Likud Bloc under the "eternal opposition leader"
Menachem Begin enjoyed a clear victory, in large part
because of support by Jews from Islamic countries. Since
that time, right-wing and left-wing governments have
alternated. In 1996, direct election of the Prime Minister
replaced election by the Knesset (Parliament) (although
only for the next three elections). Any political reform
thus far was unable to prevent a plethora of parties and
resulting instability in the political system. This polar-
ization reflects a deeply divided society.

Only about one-quarter of the Israeli people consider
themselves religious. This sector is itself extremely het-
erogeneous. It comprises militant anti-Zionists who can
only embrace a Jewish state in the Messianic Age, apo-
litical ultraorthodox Jews, moderate religious intellectuals who are prepared to accept land compromises, and

the settler movement along with its supporters. The latter group within Zionism has been growing steadily since the 1970s, as is evident in the radicalization of the formerly moderate National-Religious Party. A significant part of the Israeli orthodoxy has pursued the path from the concept of the Holy Land to that of a Holy State that could usher in a Messianic Age. The most important development in the religious array of parties of the 1990s, however, was the meteoric rise of the religious Shas party, which claims to safeguard the interests of the lower socioeconomic groups, particularly of North African Jews, not merely in religious matters.

In regard to religion, Israeli society is a study in contradictions. Israel was the first western country to have a female Prime Minister, yet many women lack rights common to other western societies because there are no civil marriage or divorce laws. Today there are probably more Talmud schools in Israel than any Jewish society of Europe ever had; at the same time, Israel occupies a leading position in gene technology and the high-tech industry. A woman wearing slacks or short sleeves cannot enter certain ultra-orthodox districts, but a transsexual female singer won a top award for Israel in the European pop music competition.

Ethiopian immigrants left their mark on Israeli society at the close of the 20th century, as have Russian immigrants. The latter are represented by their own political parties. In contrast to the early Zionists, who usually relegated the culture of their countries of origin

to the background and wanted to break away from their
Jewish Diaspora identity, a different attitude prevails
fifty years after the founding of the state. Since Jews in
their countries of origin, especially the Soviet Union,
were barely conversant in Jewish culture, and Zionist
activities were forbidden there, they view Israel as a welcome haven, but devoid of the same ideological significance. Hence it is less problematic for them to continue
identifying with the language and culture of their origins. In the course of their social and political emancipation, the Jews of Northern African and Near Eastern
descent have become ever more aware of their traditions
and try to foster them in Israel today more strongly
than was previously possible for them.

In addition to political, religious, and cultural diversi-
ty in Israeli society, the escalating conflict in the Middle
East has had a detrimental effect on the relationship
between Jewish and Arab Israelis. The nearly 20 percent
of Israelis who are Arab (of whom 78 percent are Muslims) have been increasing their solidarity with the
Palestinians in the areas that are occupied by Israel, and
are calling for equal rights in Israel, not just according
to the letter of the law, but in social reality. Moreover,
the divergent collective memory of the two population
groups is becoming more and more blatant. What some
celebrate as their day of independence, others mark as a
time of grief by calling it *nakba* (national catastrophe).
The accompanying ceremonies on the Arab side that
feature a public sounding of sirens accompanied by

moments of silence clearly demonstrate that this term is mimetic of the memorialization of the collective Jewish tragedy, the Shoah. The struggle for political recognition in the future is thus also a contest centering on sufferings of the past.

Many Jewish intellectuals in Israel have also begun to move away from the classic ideal of the liberal "Jewish state." Some of them defend the State of Israel in its basic conception as the sole Jewish state facing numerous Arab countries and as the only secure refuge for Jews threatened by persecution; others call for a "state of all citizens," which would have to relinquish everything that constitutes its Jewish definition: the Star of David in the flag, the national hymn that tells of the "Jewish soul," the Law of Return for Jews throughout the world, and the undisputed dominance of Jewish politicians.

Israel without Zionism?

If these demands were met, a new post-Zionist age in Israel would commence. Devout Zionists on the other end of the ideological spectrum contend that the task of Zionism is far from complete, since most Jews continue to live outside of the State of Israel, and even the Jewish state envisioned by Herzl did not carry out his dream of eliminating antisemitism. Just the opposite is true: anti-Zionism frequently fuels a modern hatred of Jews.

Nonetheless, for many Israelis the question remains

whether traditional Zionism has not played out its historical role by achieving a Jewish majority in Palestine and founding the State of Israel. Thus, the former Justice Minister Yossi Beilin has recommended dissolving the World Zionist Organization, and the philosopher Menachem Brinker has assessed the situation as follows: "The task of Zionism is very nearly completed. That is to say, the problem that Zionism set out to address is just about solved. Soon we will be living in a post-Zionist era, and there will no longer be a good reason for a Zionist movement to exist alongside the State of Israel. That prospect need not sadden anyone."[67] According to Brinker, Zionism deserves a place of honor in the gallery of historical developments, but not in the present. For Amos Elon, the Israeli journalist and biographer of Herzl, the Herzlian variety of Zionism is simply outdated: "Today ...there is need to move ahead to a more Western, more pluralistic, less 'ideological' form of patriotism and citizenship."[68]

"If you will it, it is no dream . . ." These are the words of Theodor Herzl's oft-cited motto. Zionism has achieved its most important goal: the establishment of a Jewish state. The foundation was a grandiose plan of a political visionary. However, the dream of secure borders, domestic peace, and neighborly co-existence is still waiting to be fulfilled.

Notes

1. *Zur Vorgeschichte des politischen Zionismus* (Vienna: Phaidon-Verlag, 1927).
2. *The Selected Writings of Mordecai Noah*, ed. Michael Schuldiner and Daniel J. Kleinfeld (Westport, Conn.: Greenwood Press, 1999), p. 107.
3. Ibid., p. 108.
4. Ibid., p. 109.
5. *The Revival of Israel: Rome and Jerusalem*, trans. Meyer Waxman, introduction by Melvin I. Urofsky (Lincoln: University of Nebraska Press, 1995), p. 43.
6. Ibid., pp. 35–36.
7. Ibid., p. 58.
8. Walther Rathenau, "Höre, Israel!" in *Impressionen* (Leipzig: Hirzel, 1902), pp. 4, 10.
9. Herzl, *Complete Diaries*, 5 vols., ed. Raphael Patai, trans. Harry Zohn (New York & London: Herzl Press & Thomas Yoseloff, 1960), vol. 1, p. 7.
10. Ibid., vol. 1, p. 7.
11. Ibid., vol. 1, p. 7.
12. Ibid., vol. 1, p. 196.
13. March 16, 1897: Herzl to Harden, in Herzl, *Briefe und Tagebücher*, vol. 4 (Berlin: Propyläen, 1990), p. 205.
14. *Theodor Herzl: A Portrait for this Age*, ed. Ludwig Lewisohn (Cleveland: The World Publishing Company, 1955), p. 193.
15. Museum of the History of Tel Aviv, Dizengoff archives.
16. *The Jewish State*, trans. Harry Zohn (New York: Herzl Press, 1970), pp. 33–34.
17. Cited in Ernst Pawel, *The Labyrinth of Exile: A Life of Theodor Herzl* (New York: Farrar, Straus and Giroux, 1989), p. 205.
18. Herzl, *Gesammelte Zionistische Werke*, vol. 5 (Berlin: Jüdischer Verlag, 1934–35), p. 463.
19. Herzl, *Complete Diaries*, vol. 1, p. 35.
20. Ibid., vol. 1, p. 38.
21. Herzl, *Jewish State*, p. 52.
22. Ibid., p. 100.

23. Ibid., p. 100.
24. Karl Kraus, "Eine Krone für Zion," in *Frühe Schriften, 1892–1900*, ed. J.J. Braakenburg, vol. 2, *1897–1900* (Munich: Kösel, 1979), pp. 304, 308.
25. Herzl, *Jewish State*, p. 33.
26. Cited in Amos Elon, *Herzl* (New York: Schocken Books, 1986), p. 226.
27. Ibid., p. 226.
28. Herzl, *Complete Diaries*, vol. 1, p. 299.
29. Ibid., vol. 2, p. 581.
30. Ibid., vol. 2, p. 581.
31. Ibid., vol. 2, p. 583.
32. Ibid., vol. 2, p. 581.
33. Ibid., vol. 2, p. 577.
34. Ahad Ha'am, *Am Scheidewege*, vol. 2 (Berlin: Jüdischer Verlag, 1913), pp. 4f.
35. Herzl, *Gesammelte Zionistische Werke*, vol. 5, p. 465.
36. Ibid., vol. 1 (Berlin: Jüdischer Verlag, 1934), pp. 188f.
37. Herzl, *Old New Land*, pp. 250–51.
38. Ahad Ha'am, *Am Scheidewege*, pp. 67, 70.
39. Arthur Ruppin, *Memoirs, Diaries, Letters*, trans. Karen Gershon, ed. Alex Bein (New York: Herzl Press, 1971), p. 83.
40. Ibid., p. 83.
41. Ibid., p. 87.
42. A.D. Gordon, *Selected Essays*, trans. Frances Burnce (New York: League for Labor Palestine, 1938; repr. New York: Arno Press, 1973), pp. 49, 50.
43. Benjamin Harshav, *Language in Time of Revolution* (Berkeley and Los Angeles: University of California Press, 1993), p. 107.
44. Gordon, Aaron David, *Erlösung durch Arbeit* (Berlin: Jüdischer Verlag, 1929), p. 83.
45. Ruppin, *Briefe, Tagebücher, Erinnerungen* (Koenigstein: Jüdischer Verlag, 1985), pp. 168f.
46. Joachim Schlör, *Tel Aviv: From Dream to City*, trans. Helen Atkins (London: Reaktion Books, 1999), p. 76, quoting Sophie Irene Loeb, *Palestine Awake: The Rebirth of a Nation* (London, n.d.), p. 27.
47. S. Yizhar (Samuel Yshar), *Mikdamot* (Tel Aviv: Zemorah-Bitan, 1992), p. 68.

48. *Jiskor: Ein Buch des Gedenkens an gefallene Wächter und Arbeiter im Lande Israel* (Berlin: Jüdischer Verlag, 1920), p. 1.

49. David Ben-Gurion, "The Imperatives of the Jewish Revolution," in Arthur Hertzberg, *The Zionist Idea* (Philadelphia: Jewish Publication Society of America, 1959), p. 607.

50. Ibid., p. 609.

51. Quoted in Yael Zerubavel, *Recovered Roots: Collective Memory and the Making of Israeli National Tradition* (Chicago: University of Chicago Press, 1995), p. 53.

52. Joseph Hayyim [Yosef Chaim] Brenner, *Mi-kan u-mi-kan* (Warsaw: Sifrut, 1911), p. 59.

53. Ibid.

54. A.D. Gordon, *Selected Essays*, p. 254.

55. Ibid., p. 254.

56. Tom Segev, *One Palestine, Complete: Jews and Arabs under the British Mandate*, trans. Haim Watzman (New York: Metropolitan Books/Henry Holt and Company, 2000), p. 462.

57. Walter Laqueur and Barry Rubin, *The Israel-Arab Reader*, 4th ed. (New York: Facts on File Publications, 1985), art. IV, p. 19.

58. Chaim Weizmann, *Trial and Error: The Autobiography of Chaim Weizmann* (New York: Harper & Brothers, 1949), p. 246.

59. Ibid., p. 246.

60. Laqueur and Rubin, *The Israel-Arab Reader*, p. 61.

61. Mark Raider, *The Emergence of American Zionism* (New York: New York University Press, 1998), p. 26.

62. G. L. Berlin, "The Brandeis-Weizmann Dispute," in Jehuda Reinharz and Anita Shapira, eds., *Essential Papers on Zionism* (New York: New York University Press, 1996), p. 340.

63. Quoted in *Israel-Arab Reader*, p. 46.

64. Ibid., p. 47.

65. Howard M. Sachar, *A History of Israel: From the Rise of Zionism to Our Time*, 2nd ed. (New York: Alfred A. Knopf, 1996), p. 203.

66. Quoted in *Israel-Arab Reader*, p. 63.

67. Menachem Brinker, "The End of Zionism? Thoughts on the Wages of Success," in Carol Diament, ed., *Zionism: The Sequel* (New York: Hadassah, 1998), p. 293.

68. Cited in Amos Elon, "Israel and the End of Zionism," in Carol Diament, ed., *Zionism: The Sequel* (New York: Hadassah, 1998), p. 301.

Suggestions for Further Reading

Almog, Shmuel. *Zionism and History: The Rise of a New Jewish Consciousness*. New York: St. Martin's, 1987.

———, Jehuda Reinharz, and Anita Shapira, eds. *Zionism and Religion*. Hanover and London: Brandeis University Press, 1998.

Avineri, Shlomo. *The Making of Modern Zionism: The Intellectual Origins of the Jewish State*. New York: Basic Books, 1981.

———. *Moses Hess: Prophet of Communism and Zionism*. New York: New York University Press, 1985.

Bauer, Yehuda. *Flight and Rescue: Brichah*. New York: Random House, 1970.

Beilin, Yossi. *His Brother's Keeper: Israel and Diaspora Jewry in the Twenty-First Century*. New York: Schocken, 2000.

Berkowitz, Michael. *Western Jewry and the Zionist Project, 1914–1933*. Cambridge: Cambridge University Press, 1997.

———. *Zionist Culture and West European Jewry before the First World War*. Cambridge: Cambridge University Press, 1993.

Cohen, Stuart. *English Zionists and British Jews: The Communal Politics of Anglo-Jewry, 1895–1920*. Princeton: Princeton University Press, 1982.

Efron, John. *Defenders of the Race: Jewish Doctors and Race Science in Fin-de-Siècle Europe*. London and New Haven: Yale University Press, 1994.

Halpern, Ben. *The Idea of the Jewish State*. Cambridge: Harvard University Press, 1961.

———, and Jehuda Reinharz. *A Clash of Heroes: Brandeis, Weizmann, and American Zionism*. New York: Oxford University Press, 1987.

Harshav, Benjamin. *Language in Time of Revolution*. Berkeley: University of California Press, 1993.

Hazony, Yoram. *The Jewish State: The Struggle for Israel's Soul*. New York: Basic Books, 2000.

Hertzberg, Arthur, ed. *The Zionist Idea: A Historical Analysis and Reader*. Philadelphia: Jewish Publication Society of America, 1959.

Koltun-Fromm, Ken. *Moses Hess and Modern Jewish Identity*. Bloomington: Indiana University Press, 2001.

Kornberg, Jacques. *Theodor Herzl: From Assimilation to Zionism*. Bloomington: Indiana University Press, 1993.

———, ed. *At the Crossroads: Essays on Ahad Ha-am*. Albany: State University of New York Press, 1983.

Laqueur, Walter. *A History of Zionism*. New York: Holt, Rinehart, and Winston, 1972.

Lavsky, Hagit. *Before Catastrophe: The Distinctive Path of German Zionism*. Detroit: Wayne State University Press, 1996.

Mandel, Neville J. *The Arabs and Zionism before World War I*. Berkeley: University of California Press, 1976.

Medoff, Rafael. *Zionism and the Arabs: An American Jewish Dilemma, 1898–1948*. Westport, Conn.: Praeger, 1997.

Mendelsohn, Ezra. *On Modern Jewish Politics*. New York: Oxford University Press, 1993.

———. *Zionism in Poland: The Formative Years, 1915–1926*. New Haven: Yale University Press, 1981.

Morris, Benny. *Righteous Victims: A History of the Zionist-Arab Conflict 1881–1999*. New York: Knopf, 1999.

Myers, David. *Re-inventing the Jewish Past: European Jewish Intellectuals and the Zionist Return to History*. New York: Oxford University Press, 1995.

O'Brien, Conor Cruise. *The Siege: The Saga of Israel and Zionism*. New York: Simon and Schuster, 1986.

Pawel, Ernst. *The Labyrinth of Exile: A Life of Theodor Herzl*. New York: Farrar, Straus, and Giroux, 1989.

Penslar, Derek. *Zionism and Technocracy: The Engineering of Jewish Settlement in Palestine, 1870–1918*. Bloomington: Indiana

University Press, 1991.

Poppel, Stephen M. *Zionism in Germany, 1897–1933: The Shaping of a Jewish Identity.* Philadelphia: Jewish Publication Society of America, 1977.

Porat, Dina. *The Blue and the Yellow Stars of David: The Zionist Leadership in Palestine and the Holocaust, 1939–1945.* Cambridge, Mass.: Harvard University Press, 1990.

Raider, Mark A. *The Emergence of American Zionism.* New York: New York University Press, 1998.

Reinharz, Jehuda. *Chaim Weizmann: The Making of a Statesman.* New York: Oxford University Press, 1993.

———. *Chaim Weizmann: The Making of a Zionist Leader.* New York: Oxford University Press, 1985.

———. *Fatherland or Promised Land: The Dilemma of the German Jew, 1893-1914.* Ann Arbor: University of Michigan Press, 1975.

———, and Anita Shapira. *Essential Papers in Zionism.* New York: New York University Press, 1996.

Robertson, Ritchie, and Edward Timms, eds. *Theodor Herzl and the Origins of Zionism.* Edinburgh: Edinburgh University Press, 1997.

Sachar, Howard. *A History of Israel.* 2d ed. New York: Alfred A. Knopf, 1996.

Schama, Simon. *Two Rothschilds and the Land of Israel.* New York: Alfred A. Knopf, 1978.

Segev, Tom. *Elvis in Jerusalem: Post-Zionism and the Americanization of Israel.* Trans. Haim Watzman. New York: Metropolitan Books, 2002.

———. *One Palestine, Complete: Jews and Arabs under the British Mandate.* New York: Metropolitan, 2000.

———. *The Seventh Million: The Israelis and the Holocaust.* New York: Hill and Wang, 1993.

Shafir, Gershon. *Land, Labor, and the Origins of the Israeli-Palestinian Conflict, 1882–1914.* Cambridge: Cambridge University Press, 1989.

Shapira, Anita. *Berl: The Biography of a Socialist Zionist*. Trans. Haya Galai. New York: Cambridge University Press, 1984.

———. *Land and Power: The Zionist Resort to Force, 1881–1948*. New York: Oxford University Press, 1992.

Shavit, Jacob. *Athens in Jerusalem: Classical Antiquity and Hellenism in the Making of the Modern Secular Jew*. London: Littman, 1997.

———. *Jabotinsky and the Revisionist Movement, 1925–1948*. London, England, and Totowa, N.J.: F. Cass, 1988.

Shimoni, Gideon. *Jews and Zionism: The South African Experience, 1910–1967*. New York: Oxford University Press, 1980.

———. *The Zionist Ideology*. Hanover: University Press of New England, 1995.

Sokolov, Nachum. *History of Zionism, 1600–1918*. Introduction by A.J. Balfour. London, New York: Longmans, Green, 1969 [orig. 1919].

Stanislawski, Michael. *Zionism and the Fin de Siècle: Cosmopolitanism and Nationalism from Nordau to Jabotinsky*. Berkeley: University of California Press, 2001.

Sternhell, Zeev. *The Founding Myths of Israel: Nationalism, Socialism, and the Making of the Jewish State*. Princeton: Princeton University Press, 1998.

Sykes, Christopher. *Crossroads to Israel, 1917–1948*. Bloomington: Indiana University Press, 1973.

Teveth, Shabtai. *Ben-Gurion: The Burning Ground, 1886–1948*. Boston: Houghton Mifflin, 1987.

Urovsky, Melvin. *American Zionism from Herzl to the Holocaust*. Garden City, N.Y.: Anchor/Doubleday, 1975.

Vital, David. *The Origins of Zionism*. Oxford: Oxford University Press, 1975.

———. *Zionism: The Formative Years*. Oxford: Oxford University Press, 1982.

Wasserstein, Bernard. *Divided Jerusalem: The Struggle for the Holy City*. New Haven: Yale University Press, 2001.

———. *Herbert Samuel: A Political Life*. Oxford: Clarendon Press, 1992.

Wheatcroft, Geoffrey. *The Controversy of Zion*. Reading: Addison-Wesley, 1997.

Zertal, Idit. *From Catastrophe to Power: Holocaust and the Emergence of Israel*. Berkeley: University of California Press, 1998.

Zerubavel, Yael. *Recovered Roots: Collective Memory and the Making of Israeli National Tradition*. Chicago: University of Chicago Press, 1995.

Zipperstein, Steven. *Elusive Prophet: Ahad Ha-Am and the Origins of Zionism*. Berkeley and Los Angeles: University of California Press, 1993.

Chronology

1825	Mordecai Manuel Noah proclaims a Jewish state in Grand Island (New York State)
1840	Damascus Affair (anti-Jewish blood libel)
1857	Rabbi Yehuda Alkalai supports the Jewish settlement of Palestine
1860	Founding of the Alliance Israélite Universelle
1862	Rabbi Zvi Hirsch Kalischer critizes the purely passive expectation of a return to Zion in the Messianic Age
1862	Moses Hess calls for the foundation of a Jewish state in *Rome and Jerusalem*
1881	Anti-Jewish pogroms in Russia following the assassination of Tsar Alexander II
1881	Beginning of the First Aliyah (emigration movement to Palestine) and the mass exodus from Eastern Europe to North America
1881	Leon Pinsker writes *Auto-Emancipation*
1882	Eliezer Ben-Yehuda emigrates to Jerusalem and has a central role in reconstructing a new Hebrew language
1882	The Biluim leave Charkov to go to Palestine
1884	The Hibbat Zion movement holds an international conference in Kattowitz
1889	Ahad Ha'am criticizes the previous colonization of Palestine in his essay "This Is Not the Way"
1892	The Austrian Jewish journalist Nathan Birnbaum is the first to use the term "Zionism"
1893	Founding of the Centralverein deutscher Staatsbürger jüdischen Glaubens as a German Jewish interest group

1894	Theodor Herzl criticizes the Viennese assimilated Jewish bourgeoisie in *The New Ghetto*
1894–95	Dreyfus Affair in Paris
1896	Theodor Herzl publishes *The Jewish State*
1897	First Zionist Congress in Basel
1897	The Algemeyner yidisher Arbeter Bund in Lite, Poyln un Rusland seeks to link Yiddish culture and socialist ideals in Eastern Europe
1901	The Jewish National Fund is created to purchase land in Palestine
1902	Herzl writes his utopian novel *Old New Land*
1902	The religious Zionist Mizrachi faction is founded
1905	After the failed Russian revolution, the Second Aliyah brings the future group of leaders to Palestine
1909	Founding of the city of Tel Aviv
1909	Founding of the Jewish defense group Hashomer
1910	Founding of the first kibbutz, Degania
1917	The Balfour Declaration "views with favour the establishment of a Jewish home in Palestine"
1917	Great Britain conquers Palestine from a disintegrating Ottoman Empire
1919	After World War I, a new beginning of immigration (Third Aliyah)
1920	The San Remo Conference assigns Palestine to the British as a League of Nations mandate and recognizes the Balfour Declaration
1920	Founding of the Histradrut (General Federation of Jewish Workers)
1921	After demonstrations on May 1, bloody riots in Jaffa and other cities
1925	Ceremonial opening of the Hebrew University in Jerusalem

1925	Beginning of the Fourth Aliyah, consisting mainly of middle-class Poles
1929	Severe Arab-Jewish clashes culminate in the Hebron massacre
1933	The Fifth Aliyah brings primarily Central European immigrants to Palestine
1937	The Peel Commission recommends a partition of Palestine
1936–39	"Arab Rebellion" of the Palestinian Arabs
1939	The British White Paper brings about drastic restrictions on emigration
1947	The United Nations General Assembly resolves to partition Palestine
1948	Founding of the State of Israel
1948–49	The War of Independence defines the borders of Israel
1956	After the Suez War, Israel has to withdraw from the conquered territories
1964	Founding of the PLO
1967	In the Six-Day War, Israel occupies the Sinai Peninsula, the Gaza Strip, and the West Bank
1973	Israel is caught off guard in the Yom Kippur War, but is able to achieve a military victory
1975	The United Nations General Assembly declares Zionism a "form of racism"
1977	Menachem Begin is the first Israeli Prime Minister to preside over a right-wing Cabinet
1979	Signing of a peace treaty between Israel and Egypt
1982	Lebanon War
1987	Beginning of "First Intifada"
1989	After the collapse of the Soviet regime, beginning of a mass emigration from Eastern Europe

1991	Iraqi missile attacks on Israeli cities in the Gulf War
1991	The Middle East Conference is convened in Madrid
1993	Historic handshake between Yitzhak Rabin and Yasir Arafat
1994	Signing of the peace accord between Israel and Jordan
1995	Signing of the interim accord between Israel and the Palestinians in Oslo
1995	Prime Minister Rabin is fatally shot by a Jewish extremist
1996	Benjamin Netanyahu defeats Shimon Peres by a narrow margin to become Israel's first directly elected Prime Minister
1998	Former Chief of Staff and Foreign Minister Ehud Barak is elected Prime Minister
2000	Failure of Camp David negotiations between Barak, Arafat, and Clinton on a Final Agreement in the region
2000	Beginning of "Second Intifada" after Ariel Sharon's visit to the Temple Mount
2001	Ariel Sharon becomes Israel's new Prime Minister and is supported by a Grand Coalition
2002	Intensification of suicide terror against Israeli civilians leads to deployment of Israeli troops in the autonomous territories and isolation of Arafat

Index of Names

About the Author

MICHAEL BRENNER is Professor of Jewish History and Culture at the University of Munich. After studying in Heidelberg and Jerusalem he received his Ph.D. from Columbia University. He has taught European Jewish history and Zionism at Indiana and Brandeis Universities, and as visiting professor at Stanford University and the Central European University in Budapest. Among his book publications are *The Renaissance of Jewish Culture in Weimar Germany* (Yale University Press, 1996, also in German and Hebrew translation), and *After the Holocaust: Rebuilding Jewish Lives in Postwar Germany* (Princeton University Press, 1997, also in German). He is co-editor of the four-volume *German-Jewish History in Modern Times* (Columbia University Press, 1996–98; also in German and Hebrew editions), *In Search of Jewish Community: Jewish Identities in Germany and Austria, 1918–1933* (Indiana University Press, 1998), *Zionistische Utopie, israelische Realität: Religion und Nation in Israel* (Munich: C.H. Beck, 1999), *Two Nations: British and German Jews in Comparative Perspective* (Tübingen: Mohr-Siebeck, 1999), and *Jewish Emancipation Reconsidered: The French and German Models* (Tübingen: Mohr-Siebeck, 2003). He serves as chairman of the Leo Baeck Institute association of historians in Germany, and is a member of the academic advisory committees of several Jewish museums and scholarly journals.

About the Translator

SHELLEY FRISCH was born and educated in New York City. She earned a doctorate in Germanic Languages and Literatures from Princeton University in 1981, and has taught German literature, film studies, and humanities at Columbia University, Haverford College, and Rutgers University. Her scholarship on exile literature has been supported by the American Council of Learned Societies, the National Endowment for the Humanities, the DAAD, and other granting institutions. She has served as executive editor of the *Germanic Review*, and has won a prestigious journalism award. Her translations from German into English include several books and numerous essays for leading newspapers and journals. She lives in Princeton, New Jersey, with her husband and their two sons.